CREATING SUCCESS
SERIES

The above titles are available from all good bookshops.

For further information on these and other Kogan Page titles, or to order online, visit **www.koganpage.com**.

How to Write Reports and Proposals

Create attention-grabbing
documents that achieve your goals

Patrick Forsyth

First published in Great Britain and the United States in 2003 by Kogan Page Limited
Fifth edition 2019

2nd Floor, 45 Gee Street
London
EC1V 3RS
United Kingdom
www.koganpage.com

122 W 27th St, 10th Floor
New York, NY 10001
USA

4737/23 Ansari Road
Daryaganj
New Delhi 110002
India

© Patrick Forsyth, 2003, 2006, 2013, 2016, 2019

The right of Patrick Forsyth to be identified as the author of this work has been asserted by him in accordance with the Copyright, Designs and Patents Act 1988.

ISBNs

Hardback   978 1 78966 003 6
Paperback   978 0 7494 8708 9
Ebook   978 0 7494 8720 1

British Library Cataloguing-in-Publication Data

A CIP record for this book is available from the British Library.

Library of Congress Cataloging-in-Publication Control Number

Names: Forsyth, Patrick, author.
Title: How to write reports and proposals : create attention-grabbing documents that achieve your goals / Patrick Forsyth.
Description: 5th Edition. | New York : Kogan Page Ltd, [2019] | Series: Creating success | Revised edition of the author's How to write reports and proposals, 2016. |
Identifiers: LCCN 2018056446 (print) | LCCN 2018057576 (ebook) | ISBN 9780749487201 (Ebook) | ISBN 9780749487089 (pbk.)
Subjects: LCSH: Business report writing. | Proposal writing in business. | Business writing.
Classification: LCC HF5719 (ebook) | LCC HF5719 .F67 2019 (print) | DDC 808.06/665–dc23
LC record available at https://lccn.loc.gov/2018056446

Typeset by Hong Kong FIVE Workshop
Print production managed by Jellyfish
Printed and bound by CPI Group (UK) Ltd, Croydon CR0 4YY

CONTENTS

PREFACE

A note on this new edition

Since this book was published in its first edition in 2003, and indeed through three further editions since then (this is the fifth), its core message has proved pretty much timeless. Reports and proposals remain an ongoing necessity of organizational life. Yet the standard of written messages in businesses and organizations remains such as to often leave something to be desired and, at worst, does harm ranging from creating simple misunderstandings to losing business or reputations. This fact creates, as this book makes clear, an opportunity for those who do a good job and write in a workmanlike way.

Ahead of getting into the core content three points are worth comment first.

Prevailing standards

The evidence of regular lack of care in writing remains all around us. When I travelled through Paddington Station in London once I saw a sign saying *Customers must stay with their luggage at all times, or they will be taken away and destroyed*. Alright, security is important, but this is silly; I hung onto to my bag tightly, I did not want to have to ring home saying I was about to be destroyed. Such examples, showing how apparently difficult it can be to write correctly, abound – a supermarket sign *Blackcurrant juice comes in two flavours – orange and strawberry*; the instructions for a refrigerator saying *The temperature control is located inside the fridge and as a safety feature can only be adjusted with the door closed*; and even a toy shop offering to include *batteries free of charge*, which may or may not be a good thing depending on how you take it (my book *Empty when half full* (Rethink Press) reviews many such examples humorously, but with a moral). Why is this so? Lack of checking, cut-and-pasting from one document to another, perhaps, but also, I think, a failure to take the writing process sufficiently seriously. If short statements like these can cause such problems then a whole report is unlikely to be automatically straightforward to write. However, any faults in prevailing standards just make something well written stand out and score points.

Electronic communication

Leaving such unintentionally humorous examples aside, one thing that has changed since publication of the first edition of this book and which continues to affect us all right now is the onward rush of electronic communication. Our love affair with email, texts, tweets and a whole range of largely truncated electronic communications tends to develop bad writing habits and this needs watching if we are to write fluently at greater length. I once saw it reported that the most common subject of emails is clarification – many are replies solely saying, in one way or another: *I'm not quite clear what you meant.* Clarity suffers and over the top brevity in many such short messages compounds the problem, as do jargon and abbreviations, especially when unexplained. A set of initials may make sense to the writer but will the reader understand?

Even when its meaning is clear the terse sentence or two that fits an email may be in a style wholly unsuited to a longer document like a report.

The broad context

Thirdly, I would make a rather different point. We live in (and this book appears in) dynamic times. Brexit, its details and aftermath, will continue to create uncertainty in the UK for a while and perhaps more widely too; indeed, many areas of the world have their problems and all such things tend to have an effect on the economy. How does that impact writing?

I suggest it does so in two ways: first, when people are under pressure, and economic and market difficulties tend to create that, they may rush through a job such as writing a report (perhaps seeing it as a chore). Yet skimping the care and attention it needs may not just create a messy report, but may affect what it is intended to do – for example, prompting people (readers) to a particular decision.

Furthermore, such macro situations in the market and economy can often (usually?) cause things to get more competitive in terms of both organizations and/or individuals. Then, any lack of clarity and precision in communicating – in, say, a sales proposal – is doubly dangerous. Good writing can differentiate – positively differentiate – just when such is needed to win business.

Looking ahead

As ever, in today's competitive workplace clear communication is a must; in its slightly revised form this book still offers solid, practical guidance to being effective when your messages must be in writing, and must work.

So, writing – good writing – can achieve a great deal for you. A moment to check what works and how to go about getting a good result is one well spent. Of course, reading a how-to book presents a challenge. However clear the principles and lessons in it are, and they are certainly intended to be clear here, they have to be related to the real world and to your own situation. With something as immediate as writing it may help to identify a document that you have written – ideally, of course, a report or proposal – and keep it by you as you read; better still this could be a draft of a document on which you are currently working. If you link advice given here to your own work, progressively making notes about it as you read, then it will help you critique both what you do and your inform people of the essentials of a technique or the key aspects of a process so that they can deploy their skills more effectively as a result of reading – and achieve improved results in their work. I intend that this book should assist in just such a way.

Introduction
Pitfalls and opportunities

In a busy business life writing anything can be a chore. There are surely more important things to be done. People to meet, decisions to be made, action to be taken. Yet all of these things and more can be dependent on written communication. A letter or memo may set up a meeting, a report may present a case and prompt a decision, a proposal may act persuasively to make sure certain action is taken or a particular option is selected.

Reading business papers can also be a chore though, and they will not achieve their purpose unless they are read, understood and do their job well enough to actively prompt the reader to action. Business writing must *earn* a reading.

You are probably both a reader and a writer of business documents. Consider writing with your reader's hat on for a moment. Do you read everything that crosses your desk? Do you read every word of the things you do read? Do you read everything from the first word through in sequence, or do you dip into things? Almost certainly the answers make it clear that not all writing is treated equally. Some documents are more likely to be read than others. Of course, some subjects demand your attention. Who ignores a personal note from the Managing Director? But the fact that some things have to be read does not make their reading any easier or more pleasurable.

Good writing, which means, not least, something that is easy to read and understand, will always be likely to get more attention than sloppy writing. Yet prevailing standards in this area are by no means universally good. I suspect that if I were given a pound for everyone in the world who, as I type this, is struggling through some document and wishing it was better written, I would not need to be writing! Something seems to happen when pen is put to paper as it were, and communications and effectiveness suffer. There is a hotel in the United Kingdom that has the following sign on the inside of every bedroom door: 'In the interests of security, please ensure that your door is fully closed when entering or leaving your room.' Just one sentence, but it is nonsense (or a good trick if you can do it), yet someone wrote this, printed and posted it and still apparently no one noticed.

Why is this? Maybe it is education; or lack of it. Certainly little I did at school assisted me with the kind of writing I found myself having to do once I was in business. Maybe it is lack of feedback; perhaps managers are too tolerant of what is put in front of them. If more of it was rejected, and had to be rewritten, then more attention might be brought to bear on the task.

Habits are important here too. We all develop a style of writing and may find it difficult to shift away from it. Worse, bad habits may be reinforced by practice. For example, in one computer company where I was asked to conduct a course on proposal writing, I was sent a number of currently typical proposals that seemed to me largely gobbledegook. I asked why they were put together as they were, and it became clear that all that had happened was that one proposal had been used as a model for the next; this had continued for six years! During that time no one had really thought about the style of document being used at all. It took a new manager to realize that the rate of strike in terms of new orders was being actively influenced for the worse by the low standard involved.

Deadly detail

We can all recognize the really bad report, without structure or style, but with an excess of jargon and convoluted sentences, and which prompts the thought: 'What is it trying to say?' But such documents do not have to be a complete mess to fail in their purpose. They are inherently fragile. One wrongly chosen word may dilute understanding or act to remove what would otherwise be a positive impression made.

Even something as simple as a spelling mistake (and, no, spell-checkers are not infallible) may have a negative effect. I will never forget, in my first year in a consulting firm, playing a small part in proposals that were submitted to a dairy products company. After meetings, deliberations and more meetings a written proposal was sent. A week passed. Then an envelope arrived from the company concerned. Inside was a single sheet of paper. It was a copy of the title page of the proposal and on it was written, in red ink the three words 'No thank you'; this alongside a red ring drawn around one typed word. The word 'dairy' had been spelt 'diary'. For a long while after that everything was checked much more carefully.

As a very first rule to drum into your subconscious – check, check and check again. I treasure the computer manual that states 'The information presented in this publication has been carefully for reliability'; no one is infallible, but I digress.

Whether the cause of a document being less good than it should be is major or minor, the damage is the same. Yet sometimes, despite recognizing poor writing when they see it, people may believe that writing habits cannot be changed. I am not sure why. I do a great deal of work in presentation skills training and people rarely doubt that that skill can be improved by training. Yet with writing they do.

A major opportunity to impress

No matter. Whatever the reasons for poor writing may be, suffice to say that, if prevailing standards are low, then there is a major opportunity here for those who better that standard. More so for those who excel. Business writing is what I call a 'career' skill. It is not only important in a job, and to the undertaking of specific tasks and the results they, in turn, produce – but it is also important to the individual. Bad reports might just come back to haunt you later and, just as with certain other skills, progress in an organization or a career may be dependent on a minimum quality of performance of such tasks.

Recently I commented on the enthusiasm of a group on an in-company course for the topic and was told by the manager who had set up the event: 'No one gets promoted in this organization unless they can make a good presentation and write a good report.' Sensible enough and, I suspect, increasingly common.

So, business writing, and particularly the writing of longer documents – the reports and proposals this book is concerned with – is a vital skill. There may be a great deal hanging on a document doing the job it is intended to do – a decision, a sale, a financial result, or a personal reputation. For those who can acquire sound skills in this area very real opportunities exist. The more you have to write, and the more important the documents you create, then the more true this is.

Quite simply, if you write well then you are more likely to achieve your business goals.

This point cannot be overemphasized. One sheet of paper may not change the world, but – well written – it can influence many events in a way that affects results and those doing the writing.

And you can write well. We may not all aspire to or succeed in writing the great novel, but most people can learn to turn out good business writing – writing that is well tailored to its purpose and likely to create the effect it intends. This book reviews some of the approaches that can make writing reports and proposals easier, quicker to execute (a worthwhile end in itself) and, most important, more likely to achieve their purpose.

Good business writing need not be difficult. It is a skill that can be developed with study and practice. Some effort may be involved, and certainly practice helps, but it could be worse. Somerset Maugham is quoted as saying: 'There are three rules for writing the novel. Unfortunately, no one knows what they are.' Business writing is not so dependent on creativity, though this is involved, and it is subject to certain rules. Rules, of course, are made to be broken. But they do act as useful guidelines and can therefore be a help. This book reviews how to go about the writing task and, in part, when to follow the rules and when to break them.

Many of the points that follow relate to both reports and proposals; any special points regarding the persuasive nature of proposals are reserved for their own chapter; and any overlap is intentional.

Confusion may occur after just a few words. What *exactly* is '24-hour service' other than insufficiently spelt out? When exactly can we expect something someone says they will do 'right away'? If this is true of such tiny communications, how much more potential for misunderstanding does a 25-page report present?

Much of the confusion arising from unclear communication is due to lack of thought. In discussion, the old adage that we should engage the brain before the mouth is a good one. Yet in conversation at least the opportunity to sort things out is there. A question can be asked, a clarification given and the conversation can then proceed with everyone clear what was meant. But with written communication the danger is that the confusion lasts. There is not necessarily an immediate opportunity to check (the writer might be 100 miles away), and a misunderstanding on page three may skew the whole message taken from an entire report.

Pitfalls: serious, and very serious

Once something is in writing any error that causes misunderstanding is made permanent, at least for a while. The dangers of ill-thought-out writing vary:

- It may be wrong, but still manage to convey its meaning. For instance, a prominently displayed sign on a golf course instructs: 'No dog walking or exercising on the course unless playing golf.' Clever dogs only? This notice may amuse, but it will probably be understood. No great harm done perhaps, though in business any fault tends to highlight the possibility of other, more serious, faults.

- It may try hard to please, yet end up giving the wrong impression. In a Renaissance Hotel I once stayed in there was a sign on the outside coffee shop tables that said:
  Courtesy of Choice: *The concept and symbol of 'Courtesy of Choice' reflect the centuries-old philosophy that acknowledges differences while allowing them to exist together in harmony.*

'Courtesy of Choice' accommodates the preferences of individuals by offering both smoking and non-smoking areas in the spirit of conviviality and mutual respect.

An absurd over-politeness just ends up making the message sound rude – this restaurant had both smoking and non-smoking areas, and if you were a non-smoker and found yourself next to a smoker, tough. It does matter.

- It may be so muddled as to confuse (and dilute the image as it does so). For example, although this comes from the past era of renting videos, Blockbuster's use of language still makes an irresistible example. This was addressed to their customers:

Limited Time Only. Rentals not returned by noon on date due shall be assessed an extended viewing fee on a per rental period basis. 5-day rentals are now 1-week rentals and if not received by noon on the 9th day shall be assessed extended viewing fee equal to the original price for each additional weekly rental period, provided that the extended viewing fee policy in participating franchise stores may vary. Membership rules apply to rental. At participating stores for a limited time. See participating stores for details and extended viewing fee policy.

Clear? I doubt it. Annoyed? Very probably. And if you run foul of the rules and then someone tells you that 'It was all made clear in writing', very annoyed, no doubt.

- It may do real damage. A press release is an important piece of writing. I noticed one quoted in the national press recently, sent out by the consulting group Accenture. The item commented that Accenture envisioned: 'A world where economic activity is ubiquitous, unbounded by the traditional definitions of commerce and universal.'

Er, yes – or rather, no. The item referred not to the content of the release, only to the fact that it contained a statement so wholly gobbledegook as to have no meaning at all. It is sad when the writing is so bad that it achieves less than nothing.

- It may just be nonsense: like the form accompanying details for those wishing to open an account with a major savings bank, which asks the applicant to specify their sex as male, female or unknown. Or the sales letter offering 'free CDs at discount prices'. Clearly an out and out mistake is recognized as just that, but its presence can reduce the overall credibility of the writer and/or their organization.

I suspect that one could extend such a list of examples extensively, right through to the language of highly abbreviated text messages. The point here is clear: it is all too easy for the written word to fail. I am sure that all the above were the subject of some thought and checking, but not enough. 'Put pen to paper' and you step onto dangerous ground.

So, the first requirement of good business writing is clarity. And I make no apology for the fact that this is returned to more than once through this book. A good report needs thinking about if it is to be clear, and it should never be taken for granted that understanding will be automatically generated by what we write.

It is more likely that we will give due consideration to clarity, and give the attention it needs to achieving it, if we are clear about the purpose of any report we may write.

Exercise

It is worth looking at your own documents (or maybe one you have designated to look at alongside reading this book as suggested) to see whether any nonsenses strike you; it is just possible that you may find some that are habits and appear regularly. If so, note and avoid them.

Why have a report?

Exactly why a report is written is important. This may seem self-evident, yet many reports are no more than something 'about' their topic. Their purpose is not clear. Without clear intentions the tendency is for the report to ramble, to go round and round and not come to any clear conclusion.

Reports may be written for many reasons, for example they may intend to:

- inform;
- recommend;
- motivate;
- prompt or play a part in debate;
- persuade;
- impress;
- record;
- reinforce or build on existing situations or beliefs;
- instruct.

In addition, they may have more complex objectives such as changing people's attitudes. Further, such factors are not mutually exclusive. You may need to do a number of things simultaneously. Or you may need to do some things for one group of people and others for different groups. A report designed to explain an organizational change, and set implementation in train, may need to pick up and develop a situation of which senior people are generally aware, yet start from scratch with others. The first group may already be persuaded that the change is good, and are eager for the details. The others may be deeply suspicious.

Any such complexity compounds the problem of writing an appropriate report. But recognizing and understanding such complexities, and seeing any inherent conflicts that may affect the way a report is received, is the first step to being able to produce something that will do the job required and do it well.

Readers' expectations

If a report is to be well received, then it must meet certain expectations of its readers. Before going into these let us consider generally what conditions such expectations. Psychologists talk about what they call 'cognitive cost'. This is best explained by example. In this book's first edition, a now-old fashioned video recorder was the obvious example, but any gadget where you might occasionally have to consult the instructions can be imagined. You turn to the appropriate page. Big mistake. You open it (try this, you can open it at random) and the two-page spread shouts at you 'This is going to be difficult!' Such a document has a high cognitive cost: rather than appearing inviting, even a cursory look is off-putting.

People are wary of this effect. They look at any document almost *expecting* reading it to be hard work. If they discover it looks easier and more inviting than they thought (a low cognitive cost), then they are likely to read it with more enthusiasm. Moreover, the effect here can be powerful: a real – perhaps surprising – clarity can score points. Reading between the lines, people take such clarity to mean a number of things: that trouble has been taken, that considerable, impressive expertise is evident.

Overall, what gives people the feeling, both at first glance and as they get further into it, that a report is not to be avoided on principle? In no particular order, readers like it if a document is:

- **Brief:** obviously something shorter is likely to appear to be easier to read than something long, but what really matters is that a report is of an appropriate length for its topic and purpose. Perhaps the best word to apply is *succinct* – to the point, long enough to say what is necessary and no more. A report may be 10 pages long, or 50, and still qualify for this description.

- **Clear:** the reader must be able to understand it. And this applies in a number of ways for example, it should be clearly written (in the sense of not being convoluted), and use appropriate language – you should not feel that, as an intended reader, you have to look up every second word in a dictionary.

- **Precise:** saying exactly what is necessary and not constantly digressing without purpose.

- **In 'our language':** in other words using a level and style of language that is likely to make sense to the average reader, and which displays evidence of being designed to do so.

- **Simple:** avoiding unnecessary complexity (something we will return to in Chapter 4).

- **Well structured:** so that it proceeds logically through a sequence that is clear and makes sense as a reasonable way of dealing with the message.

- **Descriptive:** again we return to this in Chapter 4, here it suffices to say that if there is a need to paint a picture the document must do so in a way that gets that picture over.

All these characteristics have in common that they can act to make reading easier. Further, they act cumulatively. That is, the more things are right in each of these ways, the clearer the overall report will be. If the impression is given that attention has *actively* been given to making the reader's task easier, so much the better.

Exercise

Both the above factors are worth personalizing to the kind of people to whom you must write. Whether this is internal (colleagues perhaps) or external (people like customers or collaborators) you need to be clear what your communications have to do and what kind of expectations exist at the other end. For example, a technical person may have different expectations from a layperson, and may be looking to check a level of detail that must exist and be clearly expressed for the report to be acceptable to him or her.

Make a list of typical recipients of your documents and what they expect, to keep by you as you write.

Readers' perspective

It follows logically from what has been said in this chapter so far that a good report must reflect the needs of the readers. Report writing cannot be undertaken in a vacuum. It is not simply an opportunity for the writer to say things as he or she wants. Ultimately only its readers can judge a report to be good. Thus their perspective is the starting point and as the report writer you need to think about who the intended readers are, how they think, how they view the topic of the report, what their experience to date is of the issues, and how they are likely to react to what you have to say. The following case study makes clear the importance of assessing your own intentions alongside the viewpoint of others before communicating.

Case study

A travel agency is essentially a service and a people business. In one particular firm, with a chain of some 30 retail outlets across several counties, business was lagging behind targets. The industry was, at the time, not in recession, rather the lag was due to competitive activity and was potentially something that a more active, sales-oriented approach could potentially cure. Initially the approach to the problem was to draw attention to the problem at every level. Memos were circulated to all staff. The figures quoted – the sales revenue planned and the amount to come from holidays, flights, etc – were substantial amounts. Even the shortfall was some hundreds of thousands of pounds.

The result? Well, certainly the sales graph did not rise. But, equally certainly, staff morale dropped. People went from feeling they worked for a successful organization to thinking it was – at worst – foundering; and feeling that the fault was being laid at their door. The figures meant little to the kind of young people who staffed the counters – being just unimaginably large numbers to which they were wholly unable to relate personally.

With the need to redress the situation becoming more urgent, a different strategy was planned. A new document was circulated (ahead of a sales conference). The large shortfall was amortized and presented as a series of smaller figures – one per branch. These 'catchup' figures were linked to what needed to be sold, in addition to normal business, in order to catch up and hit target. It amounted, if I remember rightly, to two additional holidays (Mum, Dad and 2.2 children) per branch, per week. Not only was this something staff could easily relate to, it was something they understood and felt was possible. Individual targets, ongoing communication to report progress and some prizes for branches hitting and beating these targets completed the picture.

What resulted this time? The numbers slowly climbed. The gap closed. Motivation increased with success in sight. And a difficult year ended with the company hitting the original planned targets – and motivation continued to run high as a real feeling of achievement was felt.

The key here was, I am sure, one of good communications. The numbers and the difficulty of hitting them did not change. But, with greater empathy with the people dealing with customers, the perception of the problem was made manageable, personal and – above all – was made to seem achievable. The results then showed that success was possible. No significant costs were involved here, just a little thought and time to make sure the communications were right, that motivation was positively affected and that results stood a real chance of rising. While this description makes it clear what the right tone of document can achieve, the details of precisely how it was written were doubtless significant too.

This links to preparation, which is dealt with in depth in the next chapter.

All this is surely no more than common sense, yet it must be easy to forget or there would not be so many turgid reports around and so many disillusioned report readers. How so?

First, it is all too easy to find you are taking a somewhat intro-spective view in putting something down on paper. After all you view yourself as important, you are involved, you are knowledge-able about the matter, why else are you the person writing the report? Secondly, many people – with you among them perhaps – have been dropped into business writing at the deep end. One day some-one requested a report, and you crept off to find something similar which you could use as a template. This is fine if what you picked up was a first-class document; if not it is like the blind leading the blind.

Powerful habits

The result of any initial bad experience may well have been to develop bad habits. The new report writer quickly gets into a par-ticular way of presenting material and much of it then becomes a reflex. This may become something that prompts failure by default. Reports fail to present a clear case, people find reading them tedious and frustrating, and whatever it is the reports aim to do (prompt a decision, perhaps) fails to occur.

Habit, and the ongoing pressure of business, combine to push people into writing on 'automatic pilot'. Sometimes if you critique something that you wrote, or that went out from your department, you can clearly see something that is wrong. A sentence does not make sense, a point fails to get across or a description confuses rather than clarifies. Usually the reason this has occurred is not that the writer really thought this was the best sentence or phrase and got it wrong. Rather it was because there was inadequate thought of any sort; or none at all.

Habits can be difficult to break and the end result can be a plethora of material moving around organizations couched in a kind of gobbledegook or what some call 'office-speak'. The exam-ple in Figure 1.1 is a caricature of this sort of communication, but there is too much that comes too close to this in circulation.

Figure 1.1   From the company notice board

STANDARD PROGRESS REPORT
(for those with no progress to report)

During the survey period which ended on 14 February, considerable progress has been made in the preliminary work directed towards the establishment of the initial activities. (*We are getting ready to start, but we have not done anything yet.*) The background information has been reviewed and the functional structure of the various component parts of the project have been matched with appropriate human resources. (*We looked at the project and decided George should lead it.*)

Considerable difficulty has been encountered in the selection of optimum approaches and methods, but this problem is being attacked vigorously and we expect the development phase will proceed at a satisfactory rate. (*George is reading the brief.*) In order to prevent the unnecessary duplication of previous work in the same field, it was necessary to establish a project team that had conducted a quite extensive tour through various departments with immediate relevance to the study. (*George and Mary had a nice time visiting everyone.*)

The Steering Committee held its regular meetings and considered quite important policy matters pertaining to the overall organizational levels of the line and staff responsibilities that devolve on the personnel associated with the specific assignments resulting from the broad functional specifications. (*Which means…?*) It is believed that the rate of progress will continue to accelerate as necessary personnel become available to play their part in the discussions that must proceed decisions. (*We really will do something soon – if we can.*)

Earning a reading

The moral here is clear. Good report writing does not just happen. It needs some thought and some effort (and some study, with which this book aims to assist). The process needs to be actively worked at if the result is going to do the job you have in mind, and do it with some certainty.

Good habits are as powerful as bad ones though. A shift from one to another is possible and the rewards in this case make the game very much worth the candle. Think what good report writing skills can achieve.

Inappropriate standard documents

Writing something, especially something you know is important and must be got right, can seem like a chore. So the ubiquitous standard letter, report or proposal is a godsend: draft it out once, store it in the computer and use it every time similar circumstances demand another such document. It saves time and money, and the mechanics of word processing allow minor changes to be made along the way, and of course the document can be – should be in many cases – personally addressed.

However, when standard text is used, and this may be for anything from acknowledging a customer enquiry or chasing a late payment to proposing something complex and important, the dangers that go along with this methodology must be considered.

Danger – again and again

While standard letters can help you run an efficient and effective business, a poor one may not just aggravate one recipient, its regular use may dilute the positive impression that it should be giving to many people over time.

Clear intention

The first prerequisite when originating anything that will become 'standard' is to have a clear intention: ask yourself what the objective is. A letter to a customer might be designed to prompt an order, or to fulfil some other purpose as you move towards that, get agreement from someone to attend a meeting with you perhaps. Whatever it is designed to do it will also project an image – for good or ill – so the language and the message must do that too. This should be very specific. It is not enough to hope that such communication will make people think well of you. What should they think? If you want to be thought efficient, project your experience or expertise or show that you understand the recipient, then a letter must be designed to do just that, and doing so becomes part of its intention.

Note: It may be useful to actually list those characteristics that you want to be on display to people 'between the lines', as it were, so that you can consciously keep them in mind as you write and actively aim to project them as appropriate.

Achieving absolute clarity

If you are absolutely clear what you are trying to do (and many such documents are not), then the next job is to ensure that what is written is clear. Achieving understanding comes first. So writing must be precise; the discount bedding retailer that told customers 'Our January Sale only happens once a year', probably did not mean to say exactly that, but no one noticed the error before their customer letter containing the phrase was sent.

Similarly, the company sending out a series of letters to late-paying customers, each more strongly worded than the last, spoilt any effectiveness they might have had by heading each one with the identical words: Final demand. Here the wrong message is inferred, just how many final demands can you have? Clearly as a customer reads letter number two they know for sure that number one manifestly did not mean what it said.

The need to do more than just be clear, perhaps to persuade, makes careful writing even more important. But clarity must always be paramount. This can be diluted by writing too fast, without due thought – or simply by failing to check once a draft is done. Often clarity fails to be achieved only by neglect. But a further good rule here is never to confuse clarity with cleverness. Ask yourself whether the brilliant pun or play on words you feel makes an exceptional heading also makes it clear what the letter is about; and edit ruthlessly to ensure clarity shines through. If a piece of text is to be reused (and reused) it is worth making sure you get it right.

Consider the apparently simple standard letter. Three things should link to rules:

- Every letter matters and if something is going to be used hundreds of times it matters more. So, what it says and how it says it are very important; standard letters must be composed with great care.

- The text should always be checked carefully, ideally by more than one person, especially if the second person is not too involved and, seeing it with fresh eyes, can act as devil's advocate.

- There should be a mandatory system of review. Once in use, every standard letter should be checked regularly. Does it still do the job for which it is intended, should it be amended or changed completely? As soon as a new standard document is originated, decide how long you can leave it and put a firm reminder in your diary (or on your computer) to check it, and then amend it if necessary, to make sure it remains one hundred per cent appropriate. You can do this with a databank of perhaps hundreds of different letters and be sure that they are all up to date all the time.

This is an area where you might prompt immediate improvement. It may well be that there are letters being sent off regularly from your organization that do not do justice to their purpose. Check. You may well find that no one has thought about some of them for a worryingly long time. If you find weak ones, rewrite them; you can do this progressively to make it manageable. Then link them into a review system and make sure that they work well, and go on working well. A final point. Standard documents sent by email are most in danger of being used inappropriately. It is seemingly all too easy to select a reply in haste that does not really suit, and in doing so dilute both image and understanding. Special care is recommended here.

Note: Though it is beyond the brief here, it seems judicious to mention that recent changes to the law about data protection mean extra care needs to be taken here with regard to communication with customers and prospects and it may be another reason to review standard text, especially if it has been used unchanged for a while.

The principles here relate to every document, perhaps more so to those more complex and longer than a letter. The final piece of the jigsaw for making standard documentation work is to amend it, at least to some degree, every time. Three kinds of alteration must be watched:

- What do you need to add?
- What do you need to omit?
- What do you need to change?

It is easy to miss things. I received a letter from a holiday company recently. One hotel was the subject and the information it gave me was good, but the name of another hotel remained unaltered from the last time the clearly standard document had been used; and in two places in as many pages. Standard documents can be a godsend, but only when they are used intelligently so that readers see them not as an inefficient time saving technique, but rather as spot on, providing the information, style and accuracy required.

The rewards of excellence

Occasionally reports may be written 'for the record'. They are of no great import or value. More often, however, if trouble is being taken to prepare a report then it has some real purpose. Reports are written to lead to action, to make things happen, or play a part in so doing. Communication influences people, and here the intention is clear: a report usually has a case to present, one that will act so as to play a part in the thinking that follows. A decision is made, albeit in part because of the way the case has been put over in a report.

So far so good, reports can influence action. But they also act to create an image of the writer. Within an organization of any size, people interact through communication. They send each other memos, they sit in meetings and on committees, they chat as they pass on the stairs, or share a sandwich at lunchtime; and all of this sends out signals. It tells the world, or at least the organization, something about them. Are they knowledgeable, competent, expert, easy to deal with, decisive – would you take their advice, follow their lead or support their cause?

All the different ways in which people interrelate act together, cumulatively and progressively, to build up and maintain an image of each individual. Some ways may play a disproportionate part, and report writing is one such. There are two reasons why this effect is important. First, reports, unlike more transient means of communication, can last. They are passed around, considered and remain on the record; more so if they are about important issues. Second, because not everyone can write a good report, people can be impressed by a clear ability to marshal an argument and put it over in writing.

Thus reports represent an opportunity, or in fact two opportunities. Reports – at least, good ones – can be instrumental in prompting action; action you want, perhaps. They are also important to your profile. They say something about the kind of person you are and what you are like to work with. In a sense there are situations where you want to make sure certain personal qualities shine through. A case may be supported by it being clear that it is presented by someone who gives attention to detail, for instance.

Longer term, the view taken of someone by their superiors may be influenced by their regularly reading what they regard as good reports. So, next time you are burning the midnight oil to get some seemingly tedious report finalized, think of it as the business equivalent of an open goal and remember, it could literally be affecting your chances of promotion!

A significant opportunity

Reports demand detailed work. Their preparation may, on occasion, seem tedious. They certainly need adequate time set aside for them. But as the old saying has it: if a job is worth doing, it is worth doing well. It may take no more time to prepare a good report than it does to prepare a lacklustre one. Indeed, the next chapter contends that a systematic approach can speed up your writing.

If reports, and other such documentation, are clear, focused and set out to earn a reading, they are more likely to achieve their purpose. In this case they are also more likely to act positively to enhance the profile of the writer. Both these results are surely worthwhile. But the job still has to be done, the words still have to be got down on paper, and faced with a blank sheet (or screen) this can be a daunting task (I know – at this point I still have six chapters in front of me!). Making writing easier starts with preparation, and it is to this we turn in the next chapter.

Summary points

- Remember that communication has inherent dangers; to be clear communication needs to be well considered.

- Reports will only achieve their purpose if the writer is clear about what he or she is seeking to achieve.

- The reader is more important than the writer; write for others, not for yourself.

- Beware old bad habits and work to establish good ones.

- Reports are potentially powerful tools – powerful in action terms and powerful in contributing to personal profile.

02
Creating a good report

Let's be formal first and define what we mean by a report.

Defining the report

A report is a written document that presents facts on its chosen topic and does so with a particular aim in mind; so a clear objective is essential. Reports are generally an aid to decision making. They can be formal or less formal, designed to fit an established format (as with a regular, say monthly, report) or they can be entirely one-off and linked to some topical topic. They can range in size from literally one page up to hundreds and have one author or many (as with a report from a committee); in the latter case a lead writer will make finalizing things easier.

There must be a very considerable number of different types of report and the intention here is to review what suits most. Just to flag some differences, reports can be the following.

Briefings	As when a manager provides a summary of the likely implications of something (eg an event or policy change and/or the questions raised by it)
The results of investigations	This might follow a formal study, as for example, with market or other research: for instance setting out what answers asking certain questions of customers or potential customers produced – and how this information might prompt action. Or it might be internal and informal, setting out information about the implications of moving offices, for example
Updates	This might summarize information on some regular basis (weekly, quarterly or whatever) in terms of any activity or its results (financial results, product sales, productivity and so on)
Discussion documents	This is normally defined as the stage before a proposal: it is essentially a document providing material for consideration or discussion (and after such review) a firm and specific proposal may follow
Proposals	The essence of this is that it is designed to persuade (more of this anon).

Beyond this the topic of a report may vary from a summary of how a particular candidate performed at a job interview to a document highlighting the best ideas from a brainstorming session or a closely argued case for taking a particular action. What is always the case is that to deserve a reading a report must have clear intentions. Given the vast range of possible reports, here the focus is on the most 'typical' kind of report (those with say 12–40 pages), though readers should bear in mind the characteristics of the reports they must write. The different arrangements of the structure of reports is dealt with in Chapter 2 and proposals separately in Chapter 6.

With something about the range of different reports established, and ahead of considering anything about the actual process of getting words onto paper, we look at the construction – the 'shape' – of a good report. There are two considerations here:

1 What makes it work for the reader?

2 What assists you to compile it quickly and easily?

Of these, the first is the most important, but the factors involved luckily act positively in both cases. The starting point to thinking here is clear.

Setting clear objectives

The most important thing to settle initially is simply *why* the report is being written. What is it *for*? Few reports are just 'about' something. They may, of course, have various intentions – to inform, motivate and so on, as mentioned in the previous chapter – but what matters most is the overall objectives. And this in turn means you must be clear what you want the end result to be after the report is delivered and read.

For example, it is unlikely to be a clear objective to write something 'about the possibility of the office relocating'. It may be valid to write something to explain why this may be necessary, compare the relative merits of different solutions and recommend the best option. Even that may need more specifics within it, spelling out the advantages/disadvantages to different groups: staff, customers etc, who may each be affected in different ways.

Objectives should be defined *from the standpoint of readers*. You need to consider:

- which particular people the report is for;
- whether the group is homogeneous or if multiple needs must be met;
- the reasons these people want or need the report;
- what they want in it, and in what detail;
- what they do *not* want;
- the result they look for (what they want to understand, what action they want to take, or what decision they want to be able to make).

It follows that it may well help to know something about the recipients of any report that you write. You may, of course, know them well; for example, they may be colleagues that you work with closely. If not, ask yourself:

- What kind of people are they (eg male/female, young/old)?
- How well do you know them?
- What is their experience of the report's topic?
- What is their level of knowledge regarding the topic?
- What is their likely attitude to it (eg welcoming/hostile)?
- What is their personal involvement (ie how do the issues affect them)?
- How do they rank the importance of the topic?
- Are they likely to find the topic interesting?
- Are they likely to act as a result of reading it?

Everything that follows, what you write, how you write it and how you arrange it, is dependent on this first premise – a clear objective is literally the foundation upon which a good report is based.

Note: In thinking about objectives it may be that you are not just making a personal decision as to what these should be. Many reports are commissioned, perhaps by your boss, so you need to know – and ask about if necessary – what their requirements are. You would not be the first person to labour to produce twenty detailed pages only to be told by someone that they expected two.

We will return to this, and to exactly how you set such an objective, in considering preparation for writing in the next chapter. Meantime we turn to the actual shape of the report itself.

A sound structure

The simplest structure one can imagine is a beginning, a middle and an end. Indeed this is what a report must consist of, but the *argument* or case it presents may be somewhat more complex. This falls naturally into four parts:

1 Setting out the situation.

2 Describing the implications.

3 Reviewing the possibilities.

4 Making a recommendation.

The two structures can coexist comfortably, as shown graphically in Figure 2.1.

Figure 2.1   The two structures of a report

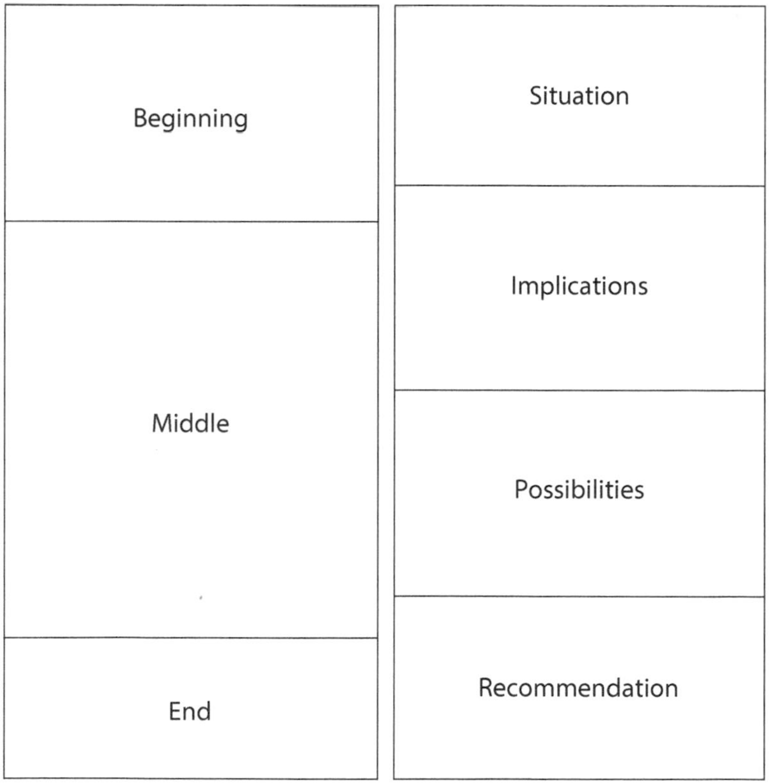

An example helps spell out the logical way an argument needs to be presented if it is to be got over clearly. Imagine an organization with certain communication problems; a report making suggestions to correct this might follow the following broad sequence:

1 *The situation*: this might refer to both the quantity and importance of written communication around, and outside, the organization. Also to the fact that writing skills were poor, and no standards were in operation, nor had any training ever been done to develop skills or link them to recognized models that would be acceptable around the organization.

2 *The implications*: these might range from a loss of productivity (because documents took too long to create and had to constantly be referred back for clarification), to inefficiencies or worse resulting from misunderstood communications. It could also include dilution or damage to image because of poor documents circulating outside the organization, perhaps to customers.

3 *The possibilities*: here, as with any argument, there might be many possible courses of action, all with their own mix of pros and cons. To continue the example, these might range from limiting report writing to a small core group of people, to reducing paperwork completely or setting up a training programme and subsequent monitoring system to ensure some improvement took place.

4 *The recommendation*: here the 'best' option needs to be set out. Or, in some reports, a number of options must be reviewed from which others can choose. Recommendations need to be specific, addressing exactly what should be done, by whom and when, alongside such details as cost and logistics.

At all stages generalizations should be avoided. Reports should contain facts, evidence, and sufficient 'chapter and verse' for those in receipt of them to see them as an appropriate basis for decision or action.

With the overall shape of the argument clearly in mind we can look in more detail at the shape of the report itself. The way in which it flows through from the beginning to the end is intended to carry the argument, make it easy to follow and to read, and to make it interesting too, as necessary, along the way.

The three parts fit, unsurprisingly, the old and useful maxim about communications, usually abbreviated to: 'Tell 'em, tell 'em and tell 'em'. In full this says: Tell people what you are going to tell them – *the introduction*; tell them in detail – *the body of the report*; and then tell them what you have told them – or *summarize*.

First, the beginning

This must start by addressing the stance of the readers. What will they be thinking as they start reading? *Will it be interesting? Readable? Will it help me? Is it important?* And will it distract them from anything else going on around them, engaging their concentration so that they give it their attention?

They have their own agenda, wanting the report to be succinct, etc, as mentioned earlier; essentially they will only give it real consideration if they find it understandable, interesting and a good fit with their situation. They do not want to find it inappropriate. It should not: confuse them, blind them with science/technicalities or jargon, lose them in an impenetrable structure (or lack of it), or talk down to them.

Judgements are made very quickly. In the first few lines a view is adopted that colours their reading of the rest of the document. First impressions last, as the old saying has it, so this stage is very important and may need disproportionate thought to get it phrased and constructed just right.

The beginning must act as an introduction, which must:

- set the scene (this can include linking to terms of reference or past discussions that prompted the report to be written);

- state the topic and theme (and maybe treatment);
- make the objectives clear;
- begin to get into the topic, creating a thread that helps draw the reader through the first part to the core of the report;
- position itself as appropriate for the readers (who must not feel they are, as it were, eavesdropping on something meant for others).

At the same time, the beginning will inevitably say something about the writer, and therefore needs to reflect anything you want readers to feel (that you are expert, professional or whatever) and not put out any untoward messages (too much jargon may say 'this person does not understand the needs of their readers'). So this element must be injected, something we return to in Chapter 4.

If it is to earn a reading, a report must get quickly to the point. This does not preclude setting the scene. A report might start: 'This report sets out to demonstrate how the organization can cut costs by 10 per cent, without sacrificing quality'. After this, and perhaps a little more, having got readers wanting to know how, it may be necessary to go back and set the scene in terms that reflect an analysis of current expenditure. But people know where the report is going – they will go through the text more easily once a desirable intention has been spelt out.

The tone of a report also needs to show itself at this first stage. Just as presenters need to establish a rapport with their audience, so a report receives continuing attention if it comes over as necessary, useful, written for a purpose, written with conviction, written by someone the reader wants to listen to, and – above all – written with understanding of, and concern for, its readers.

Get off to a good start and any continuing task is then often easier. This certainly applies to writing. Feeling you have got a good beginning breeds confidence in what must follow. And so too with reading: if a document starts well, people read on, wanting the rest to match the early acceptability. There are plenty of frustrations in corporate life; something that looks set to make life a little easier is very soon recognized and appreciated.

One of the reasons that what is often called the executive summary (a summary that is placed at the beginning rather than the end) often works well, is that it meets many of the criteria for the beginning now stated. It interests the reader who then reads on to discover the detail and see how and why the stated conclusions have been arrived at. The question of summaries is reviewed further in Chapter 6.

The middle

This is the core of the document. It is where the greatest amount of the content is to be found, and hence it has the greatest need for structure and organization. The key aims here are to:

- put over the detail of the report's message;
- maintain, indeed develop, interest;
- ensure clarity and a manner appropriate to the reader.

It may be necessary to go further. It is here that the report may seek acceptance and, conversely, set out to counter people disagreeing with or rejecting what it has to say. At the same time any complexity must be kept manageable. Doing this necessitates the simple practice of taking one point at a time. So here, attempting to practise what I preach, are a number of points all aimed at keeping this core section on track.

Putting over the content

- *A logical structure*: selecting, and describing to your readers, a way through the content (eg describing something in chronological order).

- *'Signposting' intentions*: knowing broadly what is coming (and why) makes reading easier. This is why many documents need a contents page, but it can also be done within the text – 'We will review the project in terms of three key factors: timing, cost and staffing. First, timing...' (perhaps followed by the heading 'Timing'). This is something that is difficult to overdo, the clarity it promotes and the feeling of having what is being read in context of what is to come is appreciated.

- *Using headings (and subheadings)*: this is not only effectively a form of signposting, it breaks up the text visually and makes it easier to work through a page (contrast the style of a modern business book, such as this, with the kind of dense textbook many of us suffered with at school).

- *Appropriate language*: this is important at every stage (see Chapter 4).

- Using graphics (visual graphic devices): this encompasses two types of factor – such things as bold type, capital letters, etc; and illustrations, including graphs, tables, charts, etc. Both promote clarity and are dealt with in Chapter 7.

Gaining acceptance

This is a discreet aim and can be assisted in a number of ways, for example:

- *Relate to specific groups*: general points and arguments may not be so readily accepted as those addressed to a specific group. There is no reason why a report cannot do both, with some paragraphs or points addressed generally and others starting: 'For those new to the organization', or '...those in the sales department...', etc.

- *Provide proof*: certainly if acceptance is desired, you need to offer something other than your say-so, especially if you could be seen as having a vested interest of some sort. So such things as opinion, research, statistics, and tests from elsewhere strengthen your case. Remember there is a link between the acceptability of the source and the force it brings to bear, so you may need to choose carefully exactly how best to make a point.

- *Anticipate objections*: there is no merit in ignoring negative points you are sure will come into readers' minds as the report is read, or they will simply invalidate what it says. Such are often better met head on, indeed signposted: 'Some will be asking how...? So in the next three paragraphs I will address exactly that.'

The middle section of a report needs to be visibly linked to the beginning and the end. It should pick up neatly from points made in the introduction, especially if they have bearing on the report's structure (which should be consistent throughout). And it should link equally neatly to the end. This means the thread of content needs to weave its way throughout the report and across the divide between the three main segments.

The end result is well described as seamless. The content – the case it presents – flows through and everything structural *supports* that rather than *competes* with it. The end result is something essentially readable, and also easy to follow.

One final point is worth adding before proceeding to deal with the end. It is sometimes a nice touch if the text towards the end of the middle acknowledges the stage that has been reached: 'Last, a final point before the summary...', as was done in this paragraph.

The end

First, some dangers:

- *Some reports seem to avoid the end*. The middle runs out of structure. It deteriorates into something that effectively keeps saying 'and another thing'. This can be distracting and annoying.
- *Avoid false endings*: I saw a report not so long ago that had the word 'finally', albeit used in slightly different ways, three times amongst the final paragraphs.

- *Beware of overshooting the structure*: wandering on beyond the last heading yet failing actually to move into the end section. This can add a paragraph or several pages, and consist of unnecessary repetition or irrelevant digression; all such is a distraction.

So what positively should you do here? The end has three particular intents:

- To reach and present a conclusion (this reflects the type of document involved and the nature of the argument that it may present).
- To pull together and summarize the content.
- To end positively, on a 'high note' or with a flourish. Or, if that is overstating it somewhat (and many reports are on routine matters rather than exciting ones), at least to end with some power and authority, rather than tail away.

Summarizing is not the easiest thing to do succinctly and effectively. Precisely because of this, it represents a particular opportunity. If it is done well, it impresses. Perversely, this may actually help in getting the report the attention it deserves. Realistically we know that many people glance at the end of a report before deciding to read it through. If the summary is a good sample of what is to come then it will reinforce that decision.

A summary develops out of the content most easily if the sequence and structure has been sensible, sound and logical. A summary is, after all, the natural conclusion of many cases. However you summarize, it is inherent to its acceptance that you keep this part of the report comparatively short. This does not necessarily mean that a summary must only be a few lines; it is often the case that a long, complex, report will need more than this by way of summary – the important thing is that the summary appears, and is, an appropriate length compared with the whole report. It is the need to make a summary brief as well as encapsulate the essence of the content and conclusions that make it difficult to compose without some consideration.

The end section is a part of the report where disproportionate time, editing and checking may be useful. Certainly it is a waste to slave at length over a long report, and then allow its effectiveness to be diluted (or at worst destroyed) by inattention to this vital stage.

After the end

It is worth noting that 'the end' may not be. In other words there may be pages that follow the summary and conclusions. Prime amongst such are appendices, which can be used to take certain discrete areas of detail out of the main core of the content. This may allow these areas to be dealt with in more detail, but the role of such pages is as much to keep the middle manageable and stop it from becoming too long and having its key arguments submerged in endless detail.

George had not been too happy to be given the job of organizing the office rearrangement, even though it was for the best of reasons; growth – and higher profit – meant accommodating more people; especially in customer services. He knew many people were a bit worried about how the changes would affect them, so, determined to get things right, he set to with a vengeance.

He was nothing if not thorough. He measured every room, he counted everything that moved and catalogued everything that did not. He mapped every electric wire and noted who used what pieces of equipment. Then he set about writing a report of his findings and suggestions.

Amazed at just how much there was to record, he had the good sense to check his draft with colleagues. They were appalled. People will react badly they suggested: 'People don't want all that detail. It took me 10 minutes to even find where I was going to sit and I still don't know why I'm moving – you need to look at it from other people's points of view.'

Chastened, George went 'back to the drawing board'. He rewrote the report, beginning with an overview of how the changes would help the organization. He set out a brief, clear description of how each department was affected, stressing the advantages. And he made clear what had to be done, by whom, and when to implement the changes.

Three weeks later, although there were, of course, some questions and a few suspicions, all concerned had been moved without a hitch and everything was running well. But it was nearly very different.

Exercise

At this point you may want to check any report of your own you have to hand. How would you define it? Does it have a clear objective? Is it arranged suitably with a clear beginning, middle and end? Does it have a clear focus on its reader(s)?

Summary points

- Every good report has clear objectives.
- The readers' perspective is more important than the writer's.
- There should be a clear, logical structure to the argument (situation, implications, possibilities, recommendations).
- There should be a clear shape to the report (beginning, middle and end).
- The end result should flow, be readable throughout and be 'seamless'.

03
Preparing to write

Next we look at how you get set to write something in a way that will be likely to make it effective, and specifically at how you start the actual process of writing. Knowing that they have to write a report can prompt different responses in different people, such as: put it off, doodle, write some central part quickly and ahead of the rest 'because I know that'. Whatever you do now, whatever your current habits are, you might want to consider the exercise below before continuing with this chapter.

Exercise

As was suggested earlier, it might be useful, at this point, to have something that you have written by you as you read on, and to think particularly about how it got written. In other words what procedure and actions, in what order, went into drafting it.
  You can do this in three ways:

- Wait until you have a drafting job to do, do it, keep a note of how you went about it and have it by you as you read on.

- Write something (or at least start to) as an exercise and use it as a guideline to your current style and practice.

- Locate something (preferably recent, so that you still have the details of it in mind) from the files, and make some notes as to how you composed it to keep by you.

Few areas of business skill can be acquired through some magic formula, and report writing is no exception. However, preparation perhaps comes close to acting in this way. It really is the foundation upon which successful report writing is based. Preparation allows you to do two things. First, to create a report not only that you feel content with, but that has a clear purpose and is regarded as useful by its readers. As has been said, the ultimate measure of a good report is whether it achieves the outcome you wish.

Second, a systematic approach to preparation and writing will save you time. This is a worthy result in its own right. Which of us does not have too much to do? When I first had to do a significant volume of writing, and thus looked into what made it work well in order to improve my own practice, the way I worked did change. It was a matter of some surprise to me that, whatever effect this may have had on what I wrote, I found I was getting my writing done more quickly. This experience has been found also by many people I have met through training on this topic; and is, I am sure, something you may find too.

In this chapter, therefore, we review the actual process of preparation and getting the words down. If this is put alongside what was covered in the previous chapter about the shape and structure of a report, then together the points covered begin to provide a blueprint to best practice. First things first. We will start with what you should not do.

Do not, faced with the task of writing what looks like being a 20-page report, get out a clean sheet of paper (or screen) and immediately start writing the first words: '1. Introduction. This report sets out…' Thinking must proceed writing.

Why this report?

Like so much in business, a report needs clear objectives. Let us be specific about that. Objectives are not what you wish to say, they are what you wish to *achieve*. Put simply, the task is not to write, say, 'about the new policy', it is to ensure people understand the proposed change and how it is intended to work. This in turn is designed to ensure people accept the necessity for it and are prompted to undertake their future work in a way that fits with the new policy.

Once this is clear in mind the writing is already likely to be easier, and we might move on to specifying that such a report needs to deal with five main topics:

- Some background to the change.

- An explanation of why it is necessary (perhaps emphasizing the good things it will lead to).

- Exactly what it is and how it works.

- The effects on the individual.

- What action people need to take.

With a more specific situation in mind (perhaps the topic you took for the exercise above), objectives can be formed precisely if, as the much-quoted acronym has it, they are SMART. That is:

- Specific.

- Measurable.

- Achievable.

- Realistic.

- Timed.

As an example, imagine you are setting up a training course on the subject of writing reports/proposals. What objectives would you set? The following follows the SMART principle:

The course should:

- Enable participants to ensure future reports are written in a way that will be seen by their readers as appropriate, informative and, above all, readable (*specific*).

- Ensure *measurable* action occurs after the session – eg future proposals might be measured by the number of recipients who subsequently confirmed agreement.

- Be appropriate for the chosen group – eg an inexperienced group might need a longer and more detailed programme than one made up of people with more experience – and thus have *achievable* objectives.

- Be not just achievable but *realistic* – eg here the time away from the job might be compared with the potential results of the course to ensure attendance was desirable.

- Be *timed*. When is the workshop? In a month or in six months' time? And how long will it last? One day? Two days? Results cannot come until it has taken place.

In addition, objectives should be phrased more in terms of readers than of the writer, and overall the following two key questions must be answered clearly:

- Why am I writing this?
- What am I trying to achieve?

To check if an answer to either is too vague to be useful, say of it 'which means that...' and see if this leads to a more specific statement. For example, you might say simply that such a course is designed to improve report-writing skills. So far so good; but what does this mean? It means that documents will be less time-consuming to prepare than in the past, more reader-oriented and more likely to achieve their objectives. This line of thinking can be pursued until objectives are absolutely clear.

Once your objectives are set satisfactorily you can proceed to the real business of getting something down on paper, though remember this does not mean starting at the beginning and writing to the end.

Research prior to preparation

It is important to ensure that you are in a position to write the report before you start. This may mean some research. On occasion this is too grand a word for it. You simply need a few moments to collect your thoughts, perhaps to pull together a number of papers and proceed with what that puts in your mind.

The danger is that this is all you do (if that) when research must actually mean something more elaborate and time-consuming. But make no mistake, if it needs to be done, it needs to be done. The time equation here is well proven, more time on research, and preparation, means less on writing – because the writing flows more smoothly. And the alternative may be a report that is less effective than you want, or which fails in its purpose.

So let us see what necessary research must be done as a specific aspect of overall preparation. The key question to start with is one of information, ask yourself:

- What do I need to know in order to write the report?

Then, to assemble the information, you need to consider sources. This may involve quite a list. So, for example, ask yourself:

- Which people do I need to consult (within and without the organization)?

- To which published or written sources do I need to refer? (These may include anything from an earlier report, a research study, a book, a magazine or just a memo.)

You may also need to put some order, and specify some order of importance, into the equation. It is certainly not suggested that the first step before writing anything is six months of talking, reading and making notes. Only a finite amount of material will be useful, but you may need to cast the net wide initially, at least in terms of considering what might be useful.

In this way you can get alongside you the information: opinion, facts, figures, notes, summaries, etc that you will need as you start to write.

Having gathered the information and screened out that which is superfluous, you need to organize it. The easiest way is to arrange it into some appropriate sub-groups: everything to do with costs, or with timing, say, depending on what the overall subject may be.

This makes the task of reviewing the material more manageable, then you can move on with a neat set of materials to hand, rather than a large, random heap.

> Mary has a report to write and a tight deadline. She knows it is important and also that she cannot do the work without some research. With other pressures looming, and the deadline ever-present, she opts for the minimum amount of prior checking and gets down to writing.
>
> Half-way through she realizes the draft is going off the rails. She has to pause to get some more references, again to talk to one or two colleagues and to spend time on the telephone to an outside agency. The result is that the writing takes place in fits and starts. The flow is difficult to sustain, and despite the right content being included, with the deadline now upon her she has to send off the document knowing that it could be better.
>
> In fact the lesson is not that some additional revisions would have helped, but that more time up front would have reduced the writing time and made the end result better, while still hitting the deadline. Next time she will know better.

A systematic approach

It is a rare person who can create a good report without making a few notes first, and frankly the complexity of many such documents demands a little more than this. Sometimes perhaps all that is necessary is a dozen words on the back of the proverbial envelope, but you need to be very sure that you are not missing anything. Unless you are thoroughly prepared, the chances are that whatever you create as your first draft will be somewhat off target, and time must then be spent tinkering and reworking to get it into order.

Another danger is compounded by deadlines. And who never has to work to tighter deadlines than they would like? Too often skimping preparation, combined with facing a pressing deadline, means that a writer must submit a report knowing that an additional review and some more editing would make it more likely to do its job well.

So, to encompass all possibilities and degrees of complexity, the following six-stage approach sets out a methodology that will cope with any kind of document (it is the way this book began life too). It is recommended only by its practicality. It works. It will make the job quicker and more certain. It can install the right habits and rapidly becomes something you can work with, utilizing its methods more or less comprehensively depending on the circumstances.

The six stages are now reviewed in turn, alongside an example. To provide an example that is straightforward and easy for everyone to relate to, imagine that you have to write something about your job. To make it more interesting, and give it a specific objective, imagine that what needs to be written is to attract internal candidates to apply for your job; because (we can imagine what we like) you are to be promoted – once a successful applicant is found.

Stage 1: listing

QUALIFICATIONS

EXPERIENCE   HEADLINE

DEPARTMENT

SIZE, PURPOSE,

KIND OF PERSON   REPUTATION,

– WHAT THEY CAN DO   DEVELOPMENTS

– WHAT THEY WILL DO

SALARY

TRAVEL   ACTION

BENEFITS   – REPLY

(EG CAR)   – CV

– PHOTO

– INTERVIEWS

– DEADLINE

SPECIAL CHARACTERISTICS

– CLEAN DRIVING LICENCE

– FLUENT FRENCH

– ABLE TO WRITE A GOOD REPORT

JOB TITLE

TRAINING   JOB OBJECTIVES

MAIN TASKS/

RESPONSIBILITIES

Stage 1: listing

This consists of ignoring all thoughts about sequence or structure, and simply listing everything – every significant point – that might be desirable or necessary to include (though perhaps bearing in mind the kind of report and level of detail involved).

This, a process that draws on what is sometimes called 'mind-mapping', gets all the elements involved down on paper. It may need more than one session to complete it; certainly you will find one thought leading to another as the picture fills out. Rather than set this out as a neat list down the page, many find it more useful to accommodate the developing picture to adopt a freestyle approach.

In this way points are noted, almost at random, around a sheet. This allows you to end up able to view the totality of your notes in one glance, so if it is necessary you should use a sheet larger than standard A4 paper. It is also best done on paper, not on screen (the next stages make clear why).

The stage 1 box relates this stage to the example to show something of what is done.

Stage 2: sorting

Next, you can proceed to rearrange what you have noted and bring some logic and organization to bear on it. This process may raise some questions as well as answer others, so it is still not giving you the final shape of the report. This stage is often best (and most quickly) done by annotating the original list. A second colour may help now as you begin to put things in order, make logical groupings and connections, as well as allowing yourself to add and subtract points and refine the total picture as you go.

The example continues in the stage 2 box.

Stage 3: arranging

This stage arranges your 'jottings' into a final order of contents, and here you can decide upon the precise sequence and arrangements you will follow for the report itself. For the sake of neatness, and thus to give yourself a clear guideline to follow as you move on, it is often worth rewriting the sheet you were left with after stage 2 (indeed, now so many people work directly with keyboard

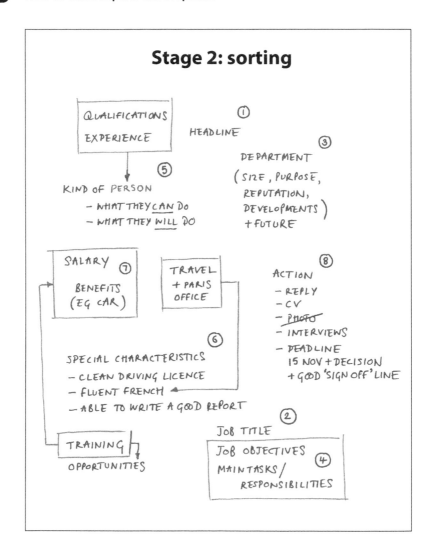

Stage 2: sorting

QUALIFICATIONS
EXPERIENCE

① HEADLINE

③ DEPARTMENT
(SIZE, PURPOSE, REPUTATION, DEVELOPMENTS)
+ FUTURE

⑤ KIND OF PERSON
– WHAT THEY CAN DO
– WHAT THEY WILL DO

⑦ SALARY
BENEFITS
(EG CAR)

TRAVEL
+ PARIS
OFFICE

⑧ ACTION
– REPLY
– CV
– PHOTO
– INTERVIEWS
– DEADLINE
  15 NOV + DECISION
  + GOOD 'SIGN OFF' LINE

⑥ SPECIAL CHARACTERISTICS
– CLEAN DRIVING LICENCE
– FLUENT FRENCH
– ABLE TO WRITE A GOOD REPORT

② JOB TITLE

TRAINING
OPPORTUNITIES

④ JOB OBJECTIVES
MAIN TASKS /
RESPONSIBILITIES

and screen, this is the point to transfer to that if you wish, as what you are creating now is a sequential list).

At this stage you can also form a view and note specifically the emphasis that will be involved. For example: What is most important? Where is most detail necessary? What needs illustrating (this may involve anything from a graph to an anecdote)? What will take most space? What, if anything, should go in an appendix?

Sometimes there is a fear that we lack material. The Board, or whoever, is expecting some quantity of analysis, consideration or thinking represented, and we worry we will have difficulty filling three pages. Usually the reverse is true. And this is the stage at which to prune, if necessary, so that what is included is well chosen, but not inappropriately long.

This is true at all levels. Contain the number of points to be made and the amount to be said about each. Of course, you need to write sufficient material to make your case, but do not risk submerging it in a plethora of irrelevant detail or subsidiary points that are actually unnecessary digressions.

The whole area of content is so important that this is commented on further in the boxed text that follows.

Deciding content and emphasis

Very often the largest problem here is deciding both what to include and not include and how much weight to give to various points. Comprehensiveness is usually not even an option. The guiding principle is *always* to focus on the reader(s). In assessing what to include ask the questions that way round:

- Do people need to know this?
- Can this be safely omitted (without diluting the argument)?
- How much do people know/understand already?
- How much more do they need to know?
- Which parts of the content need most emphasis (and detail)?
- What logical sequence will make most sense to reader(s)?
- Of course your perception is important too, but only in context of what you are trying to achieve, who you are writing for and their situation.

One other factor to bear in mind here, and through stages 2 and 3 here, is length. Think about what is appropriate and necessary; remember that, while the document must do its job, most often shorter rather than longer will be most appreciated. *Note:* If you are charged with writing a report by someone else, always ask what length is expected and be prepared to negotiate if you believe strongly that something longer or shorter is necessary or better.

Exercise

This is a good point to check, again, any report of your own that you are critiquing alongside your reading.

Stage 4: review

At this point have a final look over what you now plan to do – review the 'arranged' guideline. It will be quicker and easier to make final amendments now than when you finally print out 20 or 30 pages of draft. It may help to 'sleep on it', carrying out a final review having distanced yourself from what you have done so far, at least for a moment. You can get so close to something that you are working hard at that you cannot see the wood for the trees. One of the things you want to be clear about is the broad picture – if this is right, then the details will slot in much more easily.

Do not worry if you still want to make amendments at this stage. Add things, delete things, move things about (rewrite your guidelines if necessary) – but make sure that when you move on to write something you do so confident that the outline represents your considered view of the content and will act as a really useful guide.

It is worth pausing here to recap, at least in terms of making a comment about the process so far. For many a document, this whole process (ie stages 1–4) will only take five or ten minutes, and that is time well spent, as it will reduce the time taken once you start to write. As you develop your own style for this sort of preparation, you will find you can shorthand the process a little, with some documents able to be written from the first freehand style list. If real complexity is involved, of course, it may take longer. It is also a procedure that works well if debate and consultation among colleagues is necessary. Stage 1 can even be done in a group with a flipchart or white board being used to collect the first thoughts.

With all that has been done in mind, it is now time to write.

Stage 5: write

What else is there to say? This stage means writing it. Leaving the details of how you use language aside (for Chapter 4), there are still in fact a few points to make here – according to my plan!

First, it is worth a word or two about method. Do you write, type or what? There may be little choice here. In many organizations the word processing computer has moved in and the secretary has moved out. You type it. This may take some getting used to, but in due course it has real advantages – at least for certain kinds of writing – and affects productivity and flexibility. Laptops have expanded the possibilities here, and everyone who travels on business can, if they wish, work on the move (some of the first draft of this book was typed, on a Sunday between two training courses in Singapore, and some on the journey there).

As a considerable doubter when all this started, it is a sign of the change that is possible that I now find it harder to write something of any length longhand than I do to type it. Despite my keyboard skills being less than perfect, my thinking is now attuned to the keyboard and screen.

What else might you do? Some still originate something like a report by writing longhand and then have someone else type it.

There is nothing wrong with that. One tip: leave plenty of space. For most ordinary mortals, not everything is perfect first time. You will want to backtrack, to make amendments, add or move sections, so give yourself room to do so with reasonable neatness – your secretary will appreciate it, and be able to work from it more quickly. You also need to have a clear way of signposting exactly how you want it arranged. It is easy enough to indicate a new paragraph, but there is a range of other factors such as bold type, indented paragraphs, and so on, that need to be specified accurately.

Alternatively, you may dictate it. With a long document this is not truly good for productivity and not everyone can keep their thoughts sufficiently straight to make it work well; but it suits some people and that is what is important. Voice recognition software is still less than perfect (though some people claim to use it successfully) – for many people the restriction on how quickly they can get things down is that of how quickly they can *decide* what to put down!

One day perhaps there will be computers so sophisticated you can simply talk to them, press a key and be delivered of the typed report just as you said it. Systems are available now that are a step in this direction. We will see; but when they work and the price is right, I will be first in line.

However you opt to work, the job is to get the words down. This is the bit with the greatest element of chore in it. But it has to be done and the guidelines you have given yourself by preparing carefully will ease and speed the process. A couple of tips may help: first, choose your moment. I certainly find there are moments when I cannot seem to... when I am unable... when it is difficult... to string two coherent sentences together end to end. There are other times when things flow – when you do not dare stop in case the flow does too, and when you cannot get the words down fast enough to keep up with your thoughts.

If possible – deadlines may have an effect here – do not struggle with the former. If the writing is really not flowing – leave things. Stop. For a moment, overnight, or while you walk around the block or make a cup of tea. Many people confirm that when the words simply will not flow, a pause helps.

But also allow sufficient time: once you are under way and words are flowing smoothly it may upset the process to leave it. If you feel you need an uninterrupted hour, or more, try to organize things that way. It may both save time in the long run and help you produce a better report.

On the other hand, do not stop when you get stuck over some – maybe important – detail. This is the second tip – do not be too distracted by small hang-ups. Say you need a heading, it must be clear, pithy and make people sit up, take notice and want to read on. You just cannot think of one. Leave it and write on. You can always come back to it (and when you do, who knows, you sometimes think of just what you want in a moment).

The danger is that instead you dither, puzzle over it, waste time, get nowhere, but get so bogged down with it that you lose everything you had in your mind about the overall shape of the report or the section of it you are working on. This is true of words, phrases, sentences and even whole sections. Mark clearly what you need to come back to (so that you never forget to check it again!).

That said, the job here is to get the whole thing down on paper. It probably will not be perfect, but you should not feel bad about that; a surprisingly small number of people can create a document word for word as they want it first time. Practice will get you closer and closer, and things you are familiar with will be easier than something that is new to you or pushes your knowledge or expertise to the limits.

Some revision is usually necessary though; hence the next stage.

Stage 6: edit

If you have prepared and written well this stage may often be comparatively simple. With something new or complex more revision is necessary. There are a number of points here that help make this stage practical but not protracted:

- If possible, leave a draft a while before re-reading it. You can get very close to something and, without a pause, start to see only what you expect (or hope) is there. It is often much quicker to finish off something in this way than trying to undertake the whole job, one stage back to back with the next.

- Read things over, out loud is best. You will hear how something sounds and that reflects what readers will feel as they read. When you do this, you will find that certain things – such as overlong sentences – jump out at you very clearly (in that case, you run out of breath). Incidentally, with virtually all writing now done on screen it is worth noting that reading off a page and a screen are very different. Understanding and retention are much less when reading on screen, so when checking your material it may be worth printing something out and seeing it in that way.

- Get a colleague to read it. A fresh look often casts light on areas you have convinced yourself are fine, for no other reason than you cannot think of a better way of expressing the material. Some people habitually do this on a swap basis. Because it is time-consuming, they ask for a view of one thing in return for doing the same for someone else. This can work well; better if you do it regularly.

- Worry about the detail. Oscar Wilde said: 'I was working on the proof of one of my poems all the morning, and took out a comma. In the afternoon I put it back.' Actually the small details are important. For example, you may create greater impact by breaking a sentence into two, with a short one following a longer one. It makes a more powerful point.

And, finally, if you are word processing on a computer, do not trust the spellchecker 100 per cent. Greater accuracy throughout most of a document is matched with a tendency towards errors in things like names. You also have to watch seemingly close words: there/their, effect/affect and the like – as these will not be flagged by most systems either (you may have picked the wrong word, but spelt it correctly).

Editing is an important stage. There is a story told of a now famous operatic singer, invited to perform at a major gala concert very early in his career. He was thrilled to be there, and flattered to find, having sung his particular aria, that he was called back for several encores. He said as much to the stage manager as he was pushed back on stage for the fourth time. 'No, no, Señor', he was told, 'I am afraid they will ask you to do it again and again – until you get it right!' So too with editing. If you need to read it over three times, so be it.

Of course, you could perhaps go on making changes for ever and finally you have to let something go. But more than one look may pay dividends, and if the end result achieves what you want then the process is justified.

We have noted that spending time on preparation will reduce writing time. Similarly it is usually more time-efficient to crack through a draft and then make some changes, rather than labour over your work trying to make every line perfect as you first write. Like much that is involved here, habit plays a part. What matters is to find an approach for working through all of this that suits you; and prompts a thorough job that produces the end result you want.

Exercise

At this point it may be worth looking back at whatever report of yours you had in mind or worked on if you paused for the exercise at the start of this chapter. Take time to revisit the preparation process, following the systematic approach now laid out. You may well find that if you go through it again you will produce a content guideline that better represents your intentions (and a clearer objective?) than was the case if your earlier method was more ad hoc.

Shaking off old habits

Writing is, as has been said, very much a question of habit. It can be difficult to get right away from what you may admit is a slightly pedestrian or formula approach even when you want to do so. One thing that may help kick start you onto a new path, one that I have found helpful in training situations, is to take a completely different approach just to make you do things differently.

This involves writing something with an, albeit inappropriate, humour to it. If you are going to make it funny, it cannot be pedestrian. You have to come at it another way and you have to use different language and vocabulary; and some adjectives. The sales letter that follows is from a training exercise; those attending a training course were asked to write something funny or silly. The topic reflects the industry involved, which was travel.

Dear Decrepit Geriatric,

Grab your readies and book now. A scintillating Spanish extravaganza awaits all those over 65 years old. For only £549.99 per person (including taxes, check in charges and two quick uses of the plane's toilet) you can fly off to the sun in a specially adapted Douglas Dakota (leased only recently from Lagos Air); and for a small additional sum you can take a suitcase, provided it weighs less than 10 kilos.

The holiday delights are legion: the hotel El Fawlty is nearly finished (the building workers are due out by the end of the month), the entertainment is lavish. We offer complimentary octogenarian hang gliding, with a small charge only for those whose wheelchairs need minding while they are aloft, high-stake poker by night and triathlon training by day. At dusk you can enjoy high-priced drinks on the terrace and watch the sun sinking below the horizon through the clouds of cement dust hanging in the air, while the local youth practice their wheelies on the road below the terrace. Don't worry, you will not be able to hear their motor bikes, the sound from the flight path drowns it out. There is food too; it's good, at least the cockroaches seem to like it.

Just complete the form below. Don't delay, do it right now, you might be dead by May. See you suckers soon.

I will not quote more, if only because it will not win any comedy awards, but you get the idea. It is only possible to write this kind of spoof letter in a language and style that is different from any normal business style. Having to do this, to concentrate on making it funny in some way, gets you out of your writing rut. It can be a useful exercise and a step to changing habits and writing more appropriately and more expressively in future.

Summary points

- Be sure why you are writing and set clear objectives.
- Bear the reader in mind throughout the process.
- Handle preparation systematically, moving from an overview of possible content to a tight guideline to follow as you write.
- Try to write uninterrupted.
- Do not be afraid to edit (or to try it out on someone else).

04
The power of language

If you undertake to engender a totality of meaning that corresponds with the cognition of others seeking to intake a communication from the content you display in a report there is a greater likelihood of subsequent action being that which you desire.

You are correct. That is not a good start. If I want to say: 'If you write well, people will understand and be more likely to react as you wish' – then I should say just that. But it makes a good point with which to start this chapter. Language and how you use it matters. Exactly how you put things has a direct bearing on how they are received; and that in turn has a direct bearing on how well a report succeeds in its objectives.

Cultivating an appropriate writing style

It is clear that language makes a difference. But this is a serious understatement; language can make a very considerable difference. And it can make a difference in many different ways, as this chapter will show.

How you write is partly taste, style and also partly habit. Unless you studied English language at college or university you may have come across little about how to write, and once in business probably did what many did and found yourself following the prevailing style. How many people faced with writing their first report, and asking what it should be like, were simply given a past one and told 'something like that'? Very many, I suspect, and often it was then a case of the blind leading the blind. It is this process that, as much as anything, has led to a continuation of a common, rather over-formal, bureaucratic style that does many a report no good. Perhaps also a question of the bland leading the bland.

How you *need* to write must stem as much as anything from the view your intended readers have of what they want to read. Or in some cases are prepared to read, because – be honest – reading some business documents is always going to be something of a chore; even reading some of those you write.

Readers' expectations

Consider four broad elements first. Readers want documents to be understandable, readable, straightforward and natural. Each of these is commented on below.

Being understandable

Clarity has been mentioned already. Its necessity may seem to go without saying, though some, at least, of what one sees of prevailing standards suggests the opposite. It is all too easy to find everyday examples of wording that is less than clear. A favourite of mine is a sign you see in some shops: 'Ears pierced while you wait'. Is there some other way? Maybe there has been a technological development of which I am unaware.

Clarity is assisted by many of the elements mentioned in this chapter, but three factors help immensely:

- Using the right words: for example, are you writing about 'recommendations' or 'options', about 'objectives' (desired results) or 'strategies' (routes to achieving objectives), and when do you use 'aims' or 'goals'?

- Using the right phrases: what is '24-hour service' exactly, other than not sufficiently specific? Ditto 'personal service'? Is this just saying it is done by people? If so it is hardly a glimpse of anything but the obvious; perhaps it needs expanding to explain the nature, and perhaps excellence, of the particular service approach.

- Selecting and arranging words to ensure your meaning is clear: for example, saying 'at this stage, the arrangement is...' implies that later it will be something else when this might not be intended. Saying something like 'people feel that...' without making clear who and how many, may leave you open to charges of exaggeration if you mean, in fact, only that 'someone once said...' Saying: 'After working late into the night, the report will be with you this afternoon', seems to imply (because of the sequence and arrangement of words) that it is the report that was working late.

While this book is not intended to teach grammar, the following section explores the issue of choosing the right words a little further and gives some more examples.

The difference a word makes

Saying something is *quite nice* is so bland that, if applied to something that is *hugely enjoyable* it understates it so much as to be almost insulting. The emphasis may be inadequate but at least the word 'nice' makes it clear that something positive is being said. Blandness is certainly to be avoided; it is unlikely to add power to your writing. Choosing the wrong word is another matter. That might confuse, upset – or worse.

The following examples are designed to show the danger. Let us start with a couple of simple everyday words: *comic* and *comical.* Mean much the same thing? Not always. Comic usually relates to or in the style of comedy, whereas comical usually means funny.

More relevant to business documents are the following:

Continuous (unbroken or uninterrupted); *continual* (repeated or recurring) – a project might be continuous (in process all the time), but work on it is more likely to be continual (unless you never sleep).

Loath, as in being *loath* to do something means reluctance, to *loathe* is to hate.

Are you *uninterested* in a proposal or *disinterested* in it? The first implies you are apathetic and care not either way, the latter means you have nothing to gain from it.

Similarly *dissatisfied* and *unsatisfied* should not be confused. They mean disappointed and needing more of something, respectively.

You might want to do something *expeditious* (quick and efficient), but saying it is *expedient* might not be so well regarded as it means only that something is convenient (not always a good reason to do anything).

Fortuitous implies something happening accidentally; it does not mean fortunate.

If you are a *practical* person then you are effective, if something is *practicable* it is merely possible to do, and *pragmatic* is something meant to be effective (rather than proven to be).

One wrong word may do damage. More, particularly when closely associated, quickly create nonsense: 'This practicable approach will ensure the practical project will be continuous, it is fortuitous that I am uninterested in it and I am sure I will not be unsatisfied to see it start.'

Of course no inaccurate use of language will help you put a message over well even if it only annoys rather than confuses. For example, saying *very unique* might do – unique means unlike anything else and cannot be qualified in this way; writing 12 noon when *noon* tells you everything you need to know; or talking about an *ATM machine* when the M stands for machine (a machine machine?). Some care, maybe even some checking or study, may be useful.

Being readable

Readability is difficult to define, but we all know it when we experience it. Your writing must flow. One point must lead to another, the writing must strike the right tone, inject a little variety and, above all, there must be a logical, and visible, structure to carry the message along. As well as the shape discussed in the previous chapter, the technique of 'signposting' – briefly flagging what is to come – helps in a practical sense to get the reader understanding where something is going. It makes them read on, content that the direction is sensible (this section starts just that way, listing points to come, of which 'readable' is the second). It is difficult to overuse signposting and it can be utilized at several levels within the text.

Being straightforward

In a word (or two) this means simply put. Follow the well-known acronym KISS – Keep It Simple, Stupid. This means using:

- *Short words*: why 'elucidate' something when you can 'explain'? Why 'reimbursements' rather than 'expenses'? Similarly, although 'experiment' and 'test' do have slightly different meanings, in a general sense 'test' may be better; or you could use 'try'.

- *Short phrases*: do not say 'at this moment in time' when you mean 'now', or 'respectfully acknowledge' something when you can simply say 'thank you for'.

- *Short sentences*: having too many overlong sentences is a frequent characteristic of business reports. Short ones are good. However, they should be mixed in with longer ones, or reading becomes rather like the action of a machine gun. Many reports contain sentences that are overlong, often because they mix two rather different points. Break these into two and the overall readability improves.

- *Short paragraphs*: if there are plenty of headings and bullet points it may be difficult to get this wrong, but keep an eye on it. Regular and appropriate breaks as the message builds up do make for easy reading.

Natural

In the same way that some people are said, disparagingly, to have a 'telephone voice', so some write in an unnatural fashion. Such a style may just be old fashioned or bureaucratic. However, it could be made worse by attempts to create self-importance, or to make a topic seem weightier than it is. Just a few words can change the tone: saying 'the writer' may easily sound pompous, for instance, especially if there is no reason not to say 'I (or me)'.

The moral here is clear and provides a guideline for good writing. Reports do need some formality, but they are, after all, an alternative to talking to people. They should be as close to speech as is reasonably possible. I am not suggesting you overdo this, either by becoming too chatty or by writing, say, 'won't' (which you might sometimes acceptably say), when 'will not' is genuinely more suitable. However, if you compose what you write much as you would say it and then tighten it up, the end result is often better than when you set out to create something that is 'formal business writing'.

All these four factors have wide influence on writing style, but they do not act alone. Other points are important. Some examples, based very much on what people say they want in what they read, are now dealt with in the following bullet points. Make your writing:

- *Brief*: the gut reaction of readers is to want a document to be brief, but it is not an end in itself – a better word would be...

- *Succinct*: this makes clear that length is inextricably linked to message. If there is a rule, then it is to make something long enough to carry the message – then stop.

- *Relevant*: this goes with the first two. Not too long, covering what is required, and without irrelevant content or digression. (*Note:* Comprehensiveness is never an objective. If your reports touched on absolutely everything then they would certainly be too long. In fact, you always have to be selective; if you do not say everything, then everything you do say is a choice – you need to make good content choices.)

- *Precise*: say exactly what you mean and get all necessary details correct. Be careful not to use words like: 'about', 'I think', 'maybe' etc when you should be using a phrase that is clearly definitive.

- *In 'our' language*: this applies in every sense. It should be pitched at the right level (of technicality or complexity). It should take account of the readers' past experience and frame of reference (which means you have to know something about what these are). It should 'ring bells with them'; indeed it commands more attention and appreciation if it gives the impression of being purposely tailored to their situation.

Readers' dislikes

Readers also have hopes that what they must read will not be:

- *Introspective*: it is appropriate in most business documents to use the word 'you' more than 'I' (or 'we', 'the company', 'the department' etc). Thus saying: 'I will circulate more detailed information soon' might be better phrased as: 'You will receive more information (from me) soon.' More so, perhaps, if you add a phrase like: 'So that you can judge for yourselves.' This approach is especially important if there is persuasion involved.

- *Talking down*: 'As an expert, I can tell you this must be avoided, you must never...' Bad start – it sounds condescending. You are only likely to carry people with you if you avoid this kind of thing. I once heard a snippet of a schools broadcast on radio and someone saying: 'Never talk down to people, never be condescending. You *do know* what condescending *means* don't you?' Enough said.

- *Biased*: at least where it intends not to be. A manager writing something to staff, setting out why they think something is a good idea, and then asking for the staff's views, may prompt more agreement than is actually felt. If views are wanted, then it is better to simply set something out and ask for comment, without expressing a positive personal view in advance.

- *Politically incorrect*: there is considerable sensitivity about this these days that should neither be ignored nor underestimated. As there is still no word that means 'he or she', some contrivance may be necessary in this respect occasionally. Similarly choice of words needs care: chair, chairman, chairwoman, chairperson, say. You should think broadly about such things: sexist language, together with inappropriate references to age, religion, ethnic origin and so on, are not just unsuitable, but can get you into serious trouble. Even minor transgressions can get people thinking of you in the wrong way. I am sure I have no need to dwell on obviously distasteful examples; even an idiot would not write in a way that insults their readers, and that phrase is (intentionally) sailing close to the wind to make a point. What needs to be done is to keep an eye on the way language is used and the way you use it. That said, I was pulled up the other day for using the expression 'manning the office'. As I meant who was on duty at what times, rather than anything to do with recruitment or selection (which the suggested alternative of 'staffing' seemed to me to imply), this seemed somewhat silly at the time. But if it matters, it matters, and while the way you write should not become awkward or contrived to accommodate such matters, some care is certainly necessary.

There is a considerable amount to bear in mind here. The focus must be on the reader throughout. However, you must not forget your own position as the writer; there are things here also that must be incorporated into the way you write.

The writer's approach

Every organization has an image. The only question is whether this just happens, for good or ill, or if it is seen as something to actively create, maintain and make positive. Similarly, every report or proposal you write says something about you. Whether you like it or not this is true. And it matters. The profile wittingly or unwittingly presented may influence whether people believe, trust or like you. It may influence how they feel about your expertise, or whether they can see themselves agreeing with you or doing business with you.

Your personal profile is not only an influence in your job, one that links to the objectives you have, but it also potentially affects your career. Surely it is unavoidable that, given the profusion of paperwork in most organizations, what you write progressively typecasts you in the eyes of others – including your boss – as the sort of person who is going places, or not. It bears thinking about.

Certainly your prevailing style, and what a particular document says about you, is worth thinking about. If there is an inevitable subtext of this sort, you cannot afford to let it go by default, you need to consciously influence it. Start by considering what you want people to think of you. Take a simple point. You want to be thought of as efficient. Then the style of the document surely says something about this. If it is good, contains everything the reader wants, and certainly if it covers everything it said it would, then a sense of efficiency surely follows.

There is a plethora of characteristics that you might want your writing to reflect. Ask yourself exactly how you want various factors to come over, for example:

- What knowledge (of the subject, the people, the situation) should be evident?

- How can your empathy with people (immediate readers or others), and/or interest in them, be shown?

- What expertise should be reflected?

- How is your confidence demonstrated (or enhanced)?
- Does what you say express appropriate clout?
- Is your case put over with honesty and sincerity?
- Do you seem reliable? (Perhaps consistent reliability is what should be evident?)
- Is your decisiveness clear?

All the above, and more, are worth considering to ascertain exactly how you achieve the effect you want. It may also be important to appear well organized, concerned with detail, or to actually position yourself in a particular role: as an advisor, say, or honest broker. Such images are cumulative. They build up over time and can assist in the establishment and maintenance of relationships. Whether such is with a colleague, a customer, or concerned with establishing with the boss that you are a good person to work with (as well as good at your work), the influence can be powerful.

Similarly you might have in mind a list of characteristics you want actively to avoid seeming to embrace. For example appearing: dogmatic, patronizing, inflexible, old fashioned, or whatever, in your job, might do you little good. Some other characteristics are sometimes to be emphasized, sometimes not. Stubbornness is a good example.

Always have your own chosen profile in mind as you write. Such images are not created in a word. There is more to appearing honest than writing: 'Let me be completely honest…' (which might actually have the effect of making alarm bells ring!). Your intended profile will come, in part, from specifics such as choice of words, but also from the whole way in which you use language. So it is to more about the use of language that we now move on.

Use of language

How language is used makes a difference to exactly how a message is received. The importance of using the right word has already been touched on, but the kind of difference we are talking about can be well demonstrated by changing no more than one word. For example, consider the first sentence after the last heading: 'How language is used makes a difference to exactly how a message is received.' Add one word... 'makes a big difference to...'

Now let us see what changing that word 'big' makes: it is surely a little different to say: 'makes a great difference...' and there are many alternatives, all with varying meaning: 'real', 'powerful', 'considerable', 'vast', 'special', 'large', 'important'.

You can doubtless think of more. In context of what I am actually saying here, 'powerful' is a good word. It is not just a question of how you use language, but what you achieve by your use of it. No report writer should be without both a dictionary and thesaurus beside his or her desk; the latter is often the most useful. And any writer should watch for occasions when a check needs to be made and take a moment to do so.

This book has the specific task of focusing on reports and proposals. There is no space for a complete run down on all aspects of grammar and punctuation, though they do, of course, matter and I will make some mention of them. I want to concentrate on those things that can help create the effect you want.

Making language work for you

I regularly see examples of business writing that are almost wholly without adjectives. Yet surely one of the first purposes of language is to be descriptive. Most writing necessitates the need to paint a picture to some degree at least. Contrast two phrases:

Smooth as silk.

Sort of shiny.

The first (used, now I think of it, as a slogan by Thai Airways) conjures up a clear and precise picture; or certainly does for anyone who has seen and touched silk. The second might mean almost anything; dead wet fish are sort of shiny, but they are hardly to be compared with the touch of silk. Further, an even more descriptive phrase may be required. I heard someone on the radio describe something as 'slippery as a freshly buttered ice-rink'. Could anyone think this meant anything other than *really, really* slippery?

The question of expectation of complexity (and cognitive cost) was mentioned earlier, and to some extent it does not matter whether a written piece is short or long; whatever it is, if it makes things effortlessly clear, it is appreciated. And if it is both descriptive and makes something easier to understand, the readers are doubly appreciative.

Clear description may need working at, but the effort is worthwhile. I recently wrote asking a meeting venue to set up for a seminar arranging a group 'in a U-shape'. When I arrived the arrangement certainly put people in a U, but did so around a boardroom-style table. But I meant a U in the sense of an open U, one that gave me the ability to stand within the U to work with delegates. If I had said that, there would have been no misunderstanding.

Description is important, but sometimes we want more than that. We want an element of something being descriptive, and also memorable. It seems to me that this is achieved in two ways: first by something that is descriptive yet unusual, secondly, when it is descriptive and unexpected.

Returning to the venue theme above, I once heard a conference executive describe, as part of an explanation about room layouts, a U-shape as being one that 'puts everyone in the front row'. That, I believe, is descriptive and memorable because, while clear, it is also an unusual way of expressing it. Such phrases work well and are worth searching for.

There are occasions where this kind of approach works well, not least in ensuring something about the writer is expressed along the way. Some phrases or passages may draw strength because readers would never feel it was quite appropriate to put it like that themselves, yet find they like reading it. There is an important lesson here. Think, really think, about the things you want to describe, find words and phrases that do the job you want, and do not limit your options by only seeing possibilities within some sort of restricted 'business language'. Of course, it might be possible to go over the top here, and some ideas you may rightly reject as too extreme. Frankly the danger of including such things inappropriately is minimal, whereas the danger of failing to include something that might make a positive difference, and bring your whole text to life, is much greater. Do not let 'automatic pilot censorship' limit the effect your writing can have on people.

Another aspect you may want, on occasion, to put into your writing is emotion. If you want to seem enthusiastic, interested, surprised – whatever – this must show. A dead, passive style: 'the results were not quite as expected; they showed that...' is not the same as one that characterizes what is said with emotion: 'you will be surprised by the results, which showed that...' Both may be appropriate on occasion, but the latter is sometimes avoided when it could add to the sense and feeling and there might be occasion to strengthen that – 'the results will amaze'.

Careful selection of language

Consider this. How often when you are searching for the right phrase do you reject something as either not sufficiently formal (or conventional)? Be honest. Many people are on the brink of putting down something that will be memorable or that will add power, and then they play safe and opt for something else. It may be adequate, but it fails to impress; it may well then represent a lost opportunity.

It pays to think outside the box, to find new words, phrases or associations that will be clear, distinctive and do a good job for you. For an example let's look back. The television series *Star Trek* is now a legend across the globe. The original series may have started slowly, but it gained cult status, spawned several spin-off series across many years and led to a series of successful films; the process still continues today. Financially it is one of the most successful such franchises ever. Yet it may be difficult now to remember how different it was at its inception from other programmes broadcast at the time. Gene Roddenberry had to find a way of pitching his programme idea to the networks: he thought he had a truly novel idea, yet knew that those he sought to persuade were conservative, picking new programmes that were actually close to something already existing – the classic known quantity.

One of the most successful series at the time was the programme *Wagon Train* – a western. But the circumstances of the characters, a tight-knit group, moving on to pastures new, with each episode involving what happens to them in the new location and with the people they meet there, were essentially similar to his idea for a space odyssey. He sold *Star Trek* by describing it as '*Wagon Train* in space'. At the time this was a well-chosen analogy that people understood and, despite the risk of backing something that was actually new and different, it was largely these four words that got him agreement to make the programme. And the rest, as they say, is history.

Just one idea and one key description can create the distinction that is required to write something memorable. Often this may be best done not by a conventional description, but by thinking of something a bit, well, different or unexpected but that makes the right point. Sometimes, so to speak, you must boldly go…

Next, we look at some things to avoid.

Mistakes to avoid

Some things may act to dilute the power of your writing. They may or may not be technically wrong, but they end up reducing your effectiveness and making your objectives less certain to be achieved. Examples are given below.

Blandness

Watch out! This is a regular trap for the business writer. It happens not so much because you choose the wrong thing to write, but because you are writing on automatic pilot without thought, or at least much thought, for the detail and make no real conscious choice.

What does it mean to say something is:

- *quite* good (or bad);
- *rather* expensive; or
- *very* slow in progress?

What exactly is:

- an *attractive* promotion? (As opposed to a profit generating one, perhaps.)
- a *slight* delay? (For a moment or a month?)

All these give only a vague impression. Ask yourself exactly what you want to express, then choose language that does just that.

'Officespeak'

This is another all too common component of some business writing, much of it passed on from one person to another without comment or change. It may confuse little, but it adds little too; other than an old fashioned feel.

Phrases such as:

- 'enclosed for your perusal' (even 'enclosed for your interest' may be unsuitable. You may need to tell them why it should be of interest; or 'enclosed' alone may suffice);
- 'we respectfully acknowledge receipt of' (why not say: 'Thank you for'?);
- 'in the event that' ('if' is surely better);

- 'very high speed operation' (fast, or state just how fast);
- 'conceptualized' (thought).

Avoid such trite approaches like the plague, and work to change the habit of any 'pet' phrases you use too easily, too often – and inappropriately.

Language of 'fashion'

Language is changing all the time. New words and phrases enter the language almost daily, often from the United States and also linked to the use of technology. It is worth watching the life cycle of such words because if you are out of step they may fail to do the job you want. I notice three stages:

1 When it is too early to use them. When they will either not be understood, or seem silly or even like a failed attempt at trendiness.
2 When they work well.
3 When their use begins to date and sound wrong or inadequate.

Examples may date too, but let me try. I twitched visibly the other day when someone on BBC Radio 4 talked about an 'upcoming' event. For me at least, this is in its early stage and does not sound right at all; 'forthcoming' will suit me well for a while longer.

On the other hand, what did we say before we said 'mission statement'? This is certainly a term in current use. Most people in business appreciate its meaning and some have made good use of the thinking that goes into producing one.

What about a word or phrase that is past its best? I would suggest a common one: 'user friendly'. When first used it was new, nicely descriptive and quickly began to be useful. Now, I suspect, with no single gadget on the entire planet not so described by its makers, it is becoming weak to say the least.

Mistakes people hate

Some errors are actually well known to most people, yet they still slip through and there is a category that simply share the fact that many people find them annoying when they are on the receiving end. A simple example is the word 'unique', which is so often used with an adjective. Unique means like nothing else. Nothing can be 'very unique' or 'greatly unique', even the company whose brochure I saw with the words 'very unique' occurring three times in one paragraph that do not in fact have a product that is more than just unique even once. Think of similar examples that annoy you and avoid them too.

Others here include the likes of:

- 'different to' (different from);
- 'less' (which relates to quantity) when number is involved; 'fewer' would be correct.

Another area for care is with unnecessary or omitted inverted commas (which are becoming a modern 'plague').

Clichés

This is a somewhat difficult one. Any overused phrase can become categorized as a cliché. Yet a phrase like 'putting the cart before the horse' is not only well known, but establishes an instant and precise vision – and can therefore be useful. In a sense people like to conjure up a familiar image and so such phrases should not always be avoided, and reports may not be the place for creative alternatives like 'spread the butter before the jam'.

Following the rules

What about grammar, syntax and punctuation? Of course they matter, so does spelling, but spellcheckers largely make up for any inadequacies in that area these days. But some of the rules are made to be broken and some of the old rules are no longer regarded as rules, certainly not for business writing.

Certain things can jar. For example:

- **Poor punctuation.** Too little is exhausting to read, especially coupled with long sentences. Too much starts to seem affected and awkward. Certain rules do matter here, but the simplest guide is probably to use punctuation to allow for breathing. We learn to punctuate speech long before we write anything, so in writing all that is really necessary is a conscious inclusion of the pauses. The length of pause and the nature of what is being said indicates the likely solution. In some ways better too much than not enough.

- **Tautology** (unnecessary repetition). This is to be avoided. The classic example is people who say, 'I, myself personally'. Do not 'export overseas', simply export; do not indulge in 'forward planning', simply plan.

- **Oxymoron** (a word combination that is contradictory). These may sound silly – 'distinctly foggy' – or be current good ways of expressing something – 'deafening silence'. Some sentences can cause similar problems of contradiction – 'I never make predictions; and I never will.'

Other things are still regarded as against the rules by purists, but work well in business writing and are now in current use. A good example here is the rule stating that you should never begin a sentence with the words 'and' or 'but'. But you can. And it helps produce tighter writing and avoids overlong sentences. But… or rather however, it also makes another point: do not overuse this sort of thing.

Another similar rule is that sentences cannot be ended with prepositions. 'He is a person worth talking to' really does sound easier on the ear than: '… with whom it is worth talking'. Winston Churchill is said to have responded to criticism about this with the famous line: 'This is a type of arrant pedantry up with which I will not put.'

Still other rules may be broken only occasionally. Many of us have been brought up never to split infinitives, and they thus come under the annoyance category most of the time. There are exceptions, however: would the most famous one in the world – *Star Trek*'s 'to boldly go where no man has gone before' – really be better as 'to go boldly...'? I do not think so.

If you want a guide to the real detail here, everything from when to put a colon and when to put a semicolon, then let me recommend some further reading. There are a plethora of 'good English' guides, many of them reference books, and something like Bloomsbury's *Good Word Guide* is certainly useful. Head and shoulders above the rest however (if that is not a cliché) – and something many people will really enjoy reading – is *English Our English*, a Penguin paperback by the late Keith Waterhouse, the novelist and newspaper columnist; it is a real guide, but it is interesting, often funny and projects a great enthusiasm for writing. I like this so much that I still include and recommend it despite it being (sadly) out of print; copies are available for a few pence online.

Style

Finally, most people have, or develop, a way of writing that includes things they simply like. Why not indeed? For example, although the rule books now say they are simply alternatives, I think that to say: 'First..., secondly... and thirdly...', has much more elegance than beginning: 'Firstly...' I am not sure why.

It would be a duller world if we all did everything the same way and writing is no exception. There is no harm in using some things for no better reason than that you like them. This is likely to add variety to your writing, and make it seem distinctively different from that of other people, which may itself be useful.

Certainly you should always be happy that what you write *sounds* right. So, to quote Keith Waterhouse: 'If, after all this advice, a sentence still reads awkwardly, then what you have there is an awkward sentence. Demolish it and start again.'

Technological dilution

As a final point let me just add a reminder about technology as mentioned in the Preface, nowadays ubiquitous emails and text messages are often written in a highly abbreviated style. Sometimes this is fine, but on other occasions (I am tempted to say often) it can cause problems and the readers' understanding is diluted or destroyed; care is always necessary. But there is also a different kind of care necessary here. You need to be sure that habits of over-abbreviation are not acquired and do not start to invade your writing indiscriminately when a greater degree of formality and certainly of precision is necessary as it is with reports and proposals.

The danger here is assiduous and powerful. Furthermore, the incidence of technology where abbreviation is necessary or easy to do increases all the time (so much so that I will resist listing recent ones). The moral is clear: a real consciousness of what can go on here is useful if you are to write well in longer documents. Do not allow inappropriate habits involving abbreviation and extreme informality (or both) to be transferred unthinkingly in a way that weakens your intention to inform and explain clearly, persuade effectively or meet whatever other objectives you may have for your more formal writing.

Exercise: Write tight

One common error, and one that it is easy to get into the habit of avoiding, is being too verbose: using more words than are necessary. To get you into the habit of reviewing this, try rewriting the following phrases and, in so doing, at least halve the number of words without diluting the sense.

- It is worth noting that writing is not something to be treated in a hasty manner, because of the fact that it has a large impact on readers' impressions. (30 words)

- George did not pay any attention to the results because he did not have very much confidence in the analytical techniques. (21 words)

- In spite of the fact that he had succeeded, it did not take very long before he was sorry that he had used so many words. (26 words)

There is of course no 'right' answer; language offers too many possibilities. But a suggested abbreviation for each appears below.

Again you might usefully look back at your own report and check the language (if you want to be really thorough read all or part of it out loud as you hear errors more easily than you see them). Look particularly for things that recur out of habit; these might range from the overuse of a single word to convoluted 'businessspeak' phrases – or more. Consider: are there lessons to be learnt?

Suggested rewrites for the questions posed above:

- Because it will shape the readers' impressions, writing should be treated seriously. (11 words)

- George ignored the results because he distrusted the analytical techniques. (10 words)

- Although he succeeded, he soon regretted using so many words. (10 words)

Note: To achieve this reduction, both abbreviation, simply removing some of the words, and rephrasing is used. It may be worth noting that one delegate on a business writing skills course I conducted reduced the last example to three words, redrafting it as 'Successful, but verbose'; one might say this is going too far and changing the sense a little, but it makes a good point.

Summary points

- Make sure what you write is not only readable, but is designed for its readers.

- Put clarity first: ensuring understanding is the foundation of good business writing.

- Remember to influence the subtext that provides an image of you, and to ensure it works as you want.

- Make language work for you; be descriptive, be memorable.

- Make your writing correct, but make it individual.

05
Making numbers clear

Acommon element within many reports and proposals is that of presenting numbers, including financial figures.

The nature of numbers and number 'blindness'

Numbers can confuse or clarify. The job is first to make sure they do not confuse when they should make things clear, though perhaps it should be acknowledged that sometimes numbers are thrown around precisely in order to confuse! For example, someone in a meeting might rattle through a mass of disparate costings in the hope that just how expensive a plan is will not be dwelt upon and a similar thing can happen in writing. Similarly, the complexity of figures may be used on a grander scale: in marketing people talk about 'confusion pricing' – a pricing structure of such complexity that it intentionally makes it difficult for a customer to undertake comparison with competitors (mobile phone tariffs are an example of this with which many people are familiar and last time I checked there were more than 800,000 different tariffs available in the UK from which to choose).

That said the concentration in this chapter is on the positive, using numbers effectively in the course of written communication. This is important because many people:

- assume numbers will confuse them; they lack skills in numeracy (finding anything from percentages to break even analysis difficult) and, because they switch off to figures, they need to be motivated to appreciate them;

- can take in things on the scale of their own bank balance, but are confused by corporate figures because of their sheer size;

- are overwhelmed by the sheer volume of figures (imagine the profusion of figures spilled out by many a computer program).

Because of this particular approaches are necessary.

Actions to avoid number blindness

The presentation of figures therefore generally needs to be well considered if it is to enhance a message. The first principles are to:

- *Select* what information is presented, focusing on key information and leaving out anything that is unnecessary. This can mean for instance that information needs to be tailored; the detailed chart included in a report may be inappropriate to use for other purposes and must be abbreviated. Many slides used as visual aids are overcomplicated when simply taken from a page in a document, and this seems especially prevalent in items involving figures.

- *Separate* information, for example into an appendix to a report, so that the main message includes only key figures, and the overall flow of the case is maintained while more details can be accessed if required.

- *Separate too* information and the calculations that arrive at it. This can be done using appendices or by such devices as boxed paragraphs in a report.

- *Select the appropriate accuracy* as you present figures. Sometimes accuracy helps understanding, or is simply important, while on other occasions it can confuse and ballpark figures suit better.

- *Repeat*: repetition helps get any message across, with numbers natural repetition – for instance, going through them verbally and issuing something in writing as well – can make all the difference.

- *Proofread*: numbers must be checked perhaps even more carefully than words in written material; remember that one figure wrongly typed might change things radically, and for the worse.

Consider an example of corporate results. Sales figures may be up, but there are a variety of ways to describe this. It might be said that:

- *Sales are up*. No detail might be necessary.

- *Sales are up about 10 per cent*. A broad estimate may be fine.

- *Sales are up 10.25 per cent*. The precise figure may be important; and note that it is nonsense to say, as is often heard: *Sales are up about 10.25 per cent* – the word *about* only goes with round figures and estimates or forecasts.

- *Sales are up about £10,000*. The financial numbers may be more important than the percentage (and can be presented with the same different emphasis as just described for percentages). In addition, what the figures refer to must be made clear. For example: *Sales of product X are up 10.25 per cent for the period January–June 2016*. Language can, of course, change all such statements – *Sales are up substantially* – maybe, as here, just by adding one word.

- *Present* information in a way that makes it easy for people to understand it, for example in graph form.

Methods of presenting numbers clearly

There are two main ways of ensuring clarity with regard to numbers.

Graphs and charts

First, it is an old saying that a picture is worth a thousand words; this principle relates directly to numbers of all sorts. A graph can convey an overall picture, one immediately understood – sometimes literally at a glance.

Often two graphs work better than one more complex one, and of course they must be set out to maximize the visibility of the information they display. Thus they need to:

- be an appropriate size;

- use different colours when possible and when this helps; carefully chosen colours too, picked to contrast one against the other;

- be suitably annotated, with thought being given to what text appears on the graph itself and what is separate (in a key at the foot of the page, perhaps);

- work effectively, or be adapted to do so, if they are to be used as visual aids, when legibility is doubly important.

Various kinds of chart and graph can be used, these include:

Tables

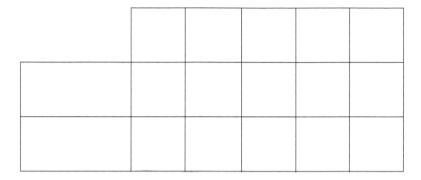

This term encompasses anything that sets out figures in columns; they can be of varying degrees of complexity.

Bar charts

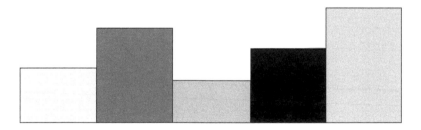

The example makes the effect of this clear; scale can again be varied for emphasis.

Pie charts

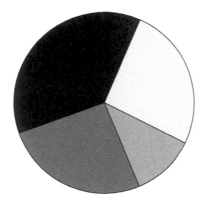

This is an especially visual device and can make many things much clearer than, say, a table and certainly a description.

Graphs

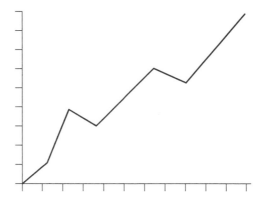

These are useful to show the differences of quantities varying over time. Care must be taken to select scales that give the picture you want (there can be a lot of trickery with this sort of graph – something to bear in mind when you are interpreting them rather than showing them).

All these devices benefit from being kept as simple as possible. Complexity, which includes trying to demonstrate too many different things (such as overall sales, sales by product, profitability and… but you take the point), can quickly drown out clarity.

Note too that sometimes a compromise is necessary here between the 'perfection' of a lovingly created graph and the time (and sometimes cost) of producing it. Despite this the greatest danger is using few, or poorly executed, devices when the information they present makes their use necessary. It can literally be true to say that one graph of some sort added to, say, a proposal, can swing an argument or get agreement to a case.

The power of such devices can be considerable. One example of information in graphic form relating to writing is to imagine a pie chart. First imagine the circle, then divide the circle into two segments, one representing how much of a message comes from the actual content and the other how much is put over by style, image and the way the profile of you the writer and your organization comes across. By linking such an empty pie chart to a particular document you can prompt consideration of how best to balance it in this respect. One graphic image can prompt considerable information and thought.

The contribution of language

Secondly, certain factors are important here with regard to the use of language:

- *Pace*: in verbal communication you may need to slow down a bit when dealing with numbers and build in more, and longer pauses; so too in writing, make sure everything is in context before figures are used or they risk simply confusing.

- *Signposting*: can focus attention and prompt concentration – *let us consider this carefully, it can be confusing and the details are important.*

- *Checks*: again in conversation an adequate number of *Is that clear?* and similar remarks or questions can help ensure people keep up; in writing more formal checks may be necessary suggesting that people pause, ensure they have everything straight so far or recap before going on.

- *Accuracy*: check carefully – numbers can be confused and you do not want to have someone thinking you offered, say, 15 per cent discount, when it was 5.

- *Precision*: exactly the right accompanying word can make a difference, ensuring that figures are taken exactly how they should be. For example: *Note that this figure is an estimate* or *This is the position today.*

- *Nonsense*: some statements using numbers can be, in effect, nonsense (as with some advertisements on the television saying things like – *now more than 70 per cent*). High percentages, of something good, may automatically sound good, but pose the question – *compared with what?* It might be a competitor, or an earlier version of the product; or it might just be unclear. Writing needs to make this clear.

Another element that can help is that of making comparisons. This can be done in various ways. For example, many numbers, not least financial ones, involve comparisons with other periods of time (eg 'this is more than last year'), or with other elements (eg 'administration costs are down, though customer service ratings are up').

Similarly, comparisons can be made simply to aid description. This is especially helpful if figures are very large or otherwise beyond the day-to-day experience of those for whom the numbers are being laid out. One aspect of this is simply in the words, describing what you want people to take on board as a serious shortfall in revenue, say, as 'akin to the national debt of most of South America'. The exaggeration is extreme and readers will recognize that this is done only to highlight the importance, and size, of the figure being discussed. Alternatively, you may select a comparison that is accurate and an important detail of what is being described. Thus an office extension might be described as 'the size of a tennis court' when even an accurate number of square metres (and this may be there too) might fail to create an easy to grasp and accurate picture.

This links to what is called *amortizing*, meaning to spread a figure expressing it as smaller units, which are divisions of the whole. For example, an annual cost of say £1,680 can be described as '£140 per month', 'only £140 per month' or 'not even £150 per month'.

The case study of the travel agent, which was set out on pages 14–15, is a good example of how the way in which figures are dealt with, and how they are made to relate to particular readers, affects the way a message is accepted and dealt with. The key here was one of communications. The numbers and the difficulty of hitting them did not change. The perception of the problem, however, was made manageable, personal and – above all – was made to seem achievable. The results then showed that success was possible. All that was necessary was to present the figures in the right way – one that reflected the realities of the situation.

Similarly, think of other numbers and how you might have to refer to them, for instance:

- Mentioning a promotional budget to the Finance Director may create objections – they see it as a large amount of money 'going out of the business'; describe it as an investment and link it tightly to the sales revenue it is designed to produce and the reaction may be different.

- A manager, working primarily to the scale of a financial year, may have to condition numbers relating to timescale when communicating with younger staff for whom long term is Friday week.

A final example will help to show the contribution of description and language to making numbers clear.

Example: Description versus numbers

Sometimes numbers need to be changed completely if they are going to make a (powerful) point. There is an old saying that you sell the sizzle and not the sausages. It recognizes that people buy what something does for or means to them; as a result, sales messages should predominantly be led by just that: a good sales person tells people what something will do for them and then shows them how.

An example of this principle in practice makes a good way of explaining how transforming numbers can empower the meaning conveyed. Consider a company making a range of cookers, grills, water heaters and other items destined for use in hotels, restaurants and various such establishments. These are products that involve some degree of technical detail, but let's concentrate on just a couple of simple facts and imagine also a busy café as the intended customer.

One feature of a flat grill is its size: one model has a cooking area of 800 square centimetres. Perhaps not many people can instantly imagine what that specific size looks like (can you?). But it was sold by describing the fact that it could cook a dozen eggs simultaneously (in other words describing what an 800 square centimetre surface area means in practical terms), and with this description linked to a mention of the 'rush at breakfast time' in the café there is likely no one in the catering business who could not call that picture instantly to mind and see the advantage. Similarly, a twin eight-pint water heater was sold not through that stark capacity description, but by referring to its ability to dispense tea and coffee at the same time.

Such descriptions focus on the situation of the customer they are directed at, and they work very well. With any number the first job is to consider – is it easy to understand, to bring to mind, to see the relevance of? And for that question to be asked not of yourself, but of those for whom you are writing because they are the people whom you must inform; transforming the number into something that does ring bells (here replacing trying to get people to imagine 800 square centimetres with their imagining a number of eggs cooking on a grill) can negate the need for elaborate explanation and paint an instantly appreciated picture.

Who is being communicated with and how numbers and financial information should be positioned always need careful consideration.

Finally, as a thought linked to language, consider two further factors:

- in verbal communication, of course, the tone of voice helps get things over – do you, for instance, want a *10 per cent increase* to *sound* good or bad? In writing you must pick introductory words and phrases to make sure it comes over as you wish;

- in written form, numbers, and the words that accompany them, can be presented with a different emphasis using graphics. In **bold type**, or *italics* perhaps, or in a larger typeface. There is also a difference between writing *10%*, *10 per cent*, or *ten per cent*; and more variations are possible. We return to graphic emphasis later.

Exercise

This is a discrete area that can be checked in the context of your own reports – if you have sections dealing with figures, financial or otherwise, read them over and make sure that how you put things is crystal clear; the possibilities for misunderstanding here are high and this needs carefully guarding against.

Summary points

Numbers can either enhance written communication or they can confuse and, at worst, result in the whole communication falling on stony ground. The key to success is to:

- recognize the role and importance of numbers within the message;
- recognize the difficulty some people have with numbers;
- choose a method of communication that highlights them appropriately, both literally (eg bold type) or by appropriate emphasis;
- illustrate figures wherever possible, for instance with graphs;
- be especially clear in what is said (or written), to use powerful description and take time for matters to be understood.

This is a vital area well worth care and thought; after all, the figures within a report may be an essential element of the whole content. If they are unclear in any way then the document may be ineffective. If they are crystal clear in say a proposal, then they may play a significant part in presenting a powerful and successful argument.

06
Making proposals persuasive

Reports can be a chore to write and a trial to get right. But proposals are a different matter, writing them makes some additional demands. How do they differ from reports? In many ways they have all the same qualities. They must earn a reading, they must hold and develop interest. They must use many of the devices already mentioned – being well structured and using language appropriately, for instance – but there is more. They must persuade, they must actively work to obtain positive decisions to do business. As such, they are a key stage in the buying/selling process, and, although this is not the place for a complete description of sales techniques, some factors are important.

A cumulative process

Selling may sometimes be a simple process consisting of one meeting. The sales person meets the buyer and, at the end of the meeting – if it has been successful – the buyer agrees to purchase and the deal is done.

Often though the process of selling something is much more complicated than this. For example, the chain of events might include the following transactions:

- Advertising and promotional activity prompt an enquiry from a prospective customer.

- That enquiry has to be handled (on the telephone, let us assume).

- The prospect is interested and asks for details to be posted (a letter and catalogue, say).

- Nothing more may be heard, but a telephone call is initiated to revive, maintain or develop the initial interest.

- At this point it may be agreed that a sales person visits to discuss matters in more detail.

- A sales meeting takes place; inconclusively.

- Follow up is again made by telephone and another meeting takes place.

- A second meeting is conducted and this time the prospect agrees to consider a proposal – 'Let's see chapter and verse in writing.'

- Once submitted, the proposal may be distributed to others around the organization.

- More chasing may be necessary, and then the potential supplier is short listed.

- Next a formal presentation is requested and made (say to the Board, or a buying committee).

- A decision to purchase (or not) is finally made.

The process might not be so drawn out, but in some cases even the example above might be a simplification. More meetings may be necessary. Certain industries demand additional stages such as a demonstration or test. And every stage, however many there are, is a form of communication. The whole process may last days, weeks, months or even years; certainly every organization has its own version of this persuasive sequence.

Now, with the kind of complexity above (and that of your own organization in mind) consider this: in terms of quality of action the process is cumulative. Prospective buyers only move from one stage to the next if they have been satisfied by the quality of what has been done to date. Thus, for example, if you send inappropriate or shoddy literature it will be more difficult to tie down a meeting.

There is another consideration here: that of strike rate. Moving right through the stages is time-consuming and expensive. Any stage poorly executed risks the process stopping there. The customer declines to continue the process (he or she may well be checking out competitors in parallel, and will continue with them) and all the time and money expended to date is wasted.

A key stage

Something of the above continuity may be true for reports also, but it is certainly very pronounced with proposals. Proposals are literally a key link in the stages of moving prospects from little or no interest in your product or service to that where they take willing, positive action to buy. What is more they are a link that comes towards the end of the sequence. By that point too much has often been done for sales to be willingly allowed to fall through by default because of poor proposals.

There is therefore a great deal hanging on proposals and they must do their job well. A proposal must not, therefore, be simply efficient and readable – it must be *persuasive*. Somehow, in many organizations, written proposals are something of a weak link. Whatever the quality of face-to-face salesmanship, it always seems to be less when something intended to be persuasive is put in writing. At worst, over-formality – often coupled with too much circumspection – dilutes the level of persuasiveness achieved.

Persuasive technique

As was said at the start of this chapter, this is no place for a complete run down on what constitutes sales technique. However, it is worth digressing briefly to consider certain essentials.

The best, and simplest, definition of selling that I know is that selling is 'helping people to buy'. This positions the whole process that demands that the seller identifies, understands and respects the buyer's needs, and makes their case act to facilitate the buyer's making a decision to buy.

Essentially selling has three tasks. To:

- create visibility (no one will buy from you if they do not know, or remember, you);

- be persuasive (make what you say understandable, attractive and credible);

- differentiate (to make your case more powerful and distinctive than those of competitors).

- All are important and often, with business justifying or necessitating a proposal stage, the third is especially so. It should never be assumed that business is not threatened by competition even when (with repeat business, for instance) this is neither in evidence nor mentioned.

The don'ts

You should not:

- *Be too clever*. It is the argument that should win the reader round, not your flowery phrases, elegant quotations or clever approach.

- *Be too complicated*. The point about simplicity has been made. It applies equally to the overall argument.

- *Be pompous*. This means saying too much about you, your organization and your product/services (instead of what it means to the reader). It means writing in a way that is too far removed from the way you would speak. It means following too slavishly the exact grammar at the expense of an easy, flowing style.

- *Over-claim.* While you should certainly have the courage of your convictions, too many superlatives can become self-defeating. Make one claim that seems doubtful and the whole argument will suffer.

- *Offer opinions.* Or at least not too many compared with the statement of facts, ideally substantiated facts.

- *Lead into points with negatives.* For example, do not say 'If this is not the case we will...', rather 'You will find... or...'

- *Assume your reader lacks knowledge.* Rather than saying, for example, 'You probably do not know that...' better to say 'Many people have not yet heard...' or 'Like others, you probably know...'

- *Overdo humour.* Never use humour unless you are very sure of its success. An inward groan as the prospect reads does rather destroy the nodding agreement you are trying to build. A quotation or quip, particularly if it is relevant, is safer and even if the humour is not appreciated, the appropriateness may be noted.

- *Use up benefits early.* A persuasive case must not run out of steam: it must end on a high note and still be talking in terms of benefits even towards and at the end.

The dos

You should do the following:

- *Concentrate on facts.* The case you put over must be credible and factual. A clear-cut 'these are all the facts you need to know' approach tends to pay particular dividends.

- *Use captions.* While pictures, illustrations, photographs and charts can often be regarded as speaking for themselves, they will have more impact if used with a caption. (This can be a good way of achieving acceptable repetition, with a mention in the text and in the caption.)

- *Use repetition.* Key points can appear more than once, for example in a leaflet and an accompanying letter, even more than once within the letter itself. This applies, of course, especially to benefits repeated for emphasis.

- *Keep changing the language.* You need to find numbers of ways of saying the same thing in brochures and letters and so on.

- *Say what is new.* Assuming you have something new, novel – even unique – to say, make sure the reader knows it. Real differentiation can often be lost, so in the quantity of words make sure that the key points still stand out.

- *Address the recipient.* You must do this accurately and precisely. You must know exactly to whom you are writing, what his or her needs, likes and dislikes are, and be ever conscious of tailoring the message. Going too far towards being all things to all people will dilute the effectiveness to any one recipient.

- *Keep the recipient reading.* Consider breaking sentences at the end of a page so that readers have to turn over to complete the sentence. (I agree, it does not look quite so neat, but it works.) Always make it clear that other pages follow, putting 'continued...' or similar at the foot of the page.

- *Link paragraphs.* This is another way to keep recipients reading. Use 'horse and cart' points to carry the argument along. For example, one paragraph starts 'One example of this is...'; the next starts 'Now let's look at how that works...'

- *Be descriptive.* Really descriptive. In words, a system may be better described as 'smooth as silk' than 'very straightforward to operate'. Remember, you know how good what you are describing is, the readers do not. You need to tell them and you must not assume they will catch your enthusiasm from a brief phrase.

- *Involve people.* First your people. Do not say '... the head of our XYZ Division'; say 'John Smith, the head of our XYZ Division'. And other people. Do not say 'it is a proven service...'; say 'more than 300 clients have found it valuable...'

- *Add credibility.* For example, if you quote users, quote names (with their permission); if you quote figures, quote them specifically; and mention people by name. Being specific adds to credibility, so do not say; 'This is described in our booklet on...', rather 'This is described on page 16 of our booklet on...'

- *Use repetition.* Key points can appear more than once, in the leaflet and the letter, even more than once within the letter itself. This applies, of course, especially to benefits repeated for emphasis. You will notice this point is repeated, either to show that the technique works or perhaps to demonstrate that some halfhearted attempts at humour are not altogether recommended!

This is a topic that ultimately overlaps with the techniques of direct mail; there are many possibilities and it is therefore something that you may conclude bears some separate study. So, although the rest of this chapter touches on some of the sales techniques, from here on it concentrates primarily on how to write proposals and the 'shape' they need to be if they are to do their job well.

Quotations versus proposals

It may be worth being clear about what exactly is meant by the two words 'proposal' and 'quotation'. Although they are sometimes used in a way that appears similar, in sales terms they each imply something very different.

Proposals have to explain and justify what they suggest. They may make recommendations, they certainly assume that their job is to persuade. Whereas quotations, which are much simpler documents, simply set out a – usually requested – option, saying if it is available and what it costs. They assume, rightly or wrongly, that the sales job is done and that persuasion is not necessary. Many quotations should have more, sometimes much more, of the proposal about them. Here the review is concerned with the more complex proposals, though the principles concerned might act to beef up a quotation.

Choice of format

There are two approaches to the format of proposals. Sometimes a letter, albeit maybe a longish one, is entirely appropriate. Indeed, sometimes doing more than this can overstate a case and put the recipient off. It is seen as over-engineering.

Alternatively what is necessary is much more like a report, though with a persuasive bent. Consider both in turn, and when and why each may be appropriate.

Letter proposals

This is simply what the name suggests. It starts with a first sheet set out like a letter, which begins 'Dear...' It may be several pages long, with a number of subheadings, but it is essentially less formal than a report-style proposal. This style is appropriate when:

- a more detailed proposal is not needed, because there would be insufficient content, or an over-formality;
- the objective (or request) is only to summarize discussions that have taken place;
- there are no outstanding issues (unsolved at prior meetings, for instance);
- there is no threat of competition.

Where these, or some of them, do not apply another approach is necessary.

Formal proposal

This is a report-style document, usually bound in some way and thus more elaborate and formal. Such is appropriate when:

- recommendations are complex;
- what is being sold is high in cost (or, just as importantly, will be seen as being so);

- there is more than one 'customer', a committee, a recommender and a decision maker acting together, or some other combination of people who need to confer and will thus see exactly the same thing;

- (linked to the previous point) you have not met some of those who will be instrumental in making the decision;

- you know you have competitors and are being compared with them.

In many businesses it is common for there to be multiple decision makers or influencers. Where this is even suspected it is wise always to ask how many copies of a proposal are required. If you have seen, say, two people and the answer is three copies, maybe there is someone else you need to be aware of and more questions (or even another meeting) become the order of the day before you move on.

In anything to do with selling, the customer and his or her views rank high. What customers want should rightly influence the kind of proposal you put in. Ask them questions such as:

- How formal should it be?
- What sort of detail is expected?
- How long should it be?
- How many people will see it?
- When do they want to receive it?

You do not have to follow their answers slavishly, but must make a considered judgement. For example, if you are dealing with people you know, they may well suggest not being too formal. But if you know you are the competition, it may still pay to do something more formal than a letter; after all, your document and someone else's will be compared alongside each other. In a comparison between a letter-style and more formal proposal, the former tends to look weaker, especially when related to value for money.

Timing

Timing is worth a particular word. It is naturally good to meet customers' deadlines, even in some cases if it means burning the midnight oil. But it may be they want your proposal to reflect your *considered* opinion. Promising that on a complex matter 'in 24 hours' may simply not be credible. Too much speed in such a case can cast doubts on quality and originality. This is especially true of services, and of anything that is effectively bespoke. So much so that it may occasionally be wise to delay something, asking for more time than you actually need to enhance the feeling of tailoring and consideration when it arrives.

So, at this stage you know something about the customer's needs, you know who is involved in the decision (ie those who will read whatever you write) and when the proposal is wanted. Remember the chapter on preparation: add on any time you will need to spend with colleagues – in discussion, brainstorming, whatever – and set aside sufficient time to do a good job. Once the document has been sent, then – for good or ill – it must stand on its own feet.

Case study

A consultant takes a careful brief. He has a good first meeting with the prospective client. A rapport is established and, at the end of the meeting he leaves, confident that the prospect believes he understands the problem; indeed this he has checked out.

He asks the necessary questions about the proposal that must now be submitted. He knows he is in competition with another supplier, that sufficient detail is necessary, and that an innovative approach is expected but one that *must* fit certain existing parameters. There is also a degree of urgency – not too much, but given the current workload...

In the event, the proposal hits the deadline, but only just. A week later the consultant receives a telephone call from the manager on whom the decision rests. He has one question of detail. He wants to check whether one element of the suggested approach made in the proposal meets one of the fixed criteria. The consultant well remembers the point, and they turn together to the relevant page. 'It's not quite clear...' says the manager; and indeed on rereading it, it is not. The wording is woolly. However, the consultant puts the matter straight, assuring the manager that the methodology is suggested that way *precisely* to meet the given criteria. This seems to settle the matter and a decision is promised in a week or so.

Seven days later a letter arrives. It is polite, it praises the approach; but it says no.

The case study makes a good point. No one can be certain that the offending paragraph was itself solely instrumental in losing the work; but it cannot have helped. There is a necessary attention to detail required here (perhaps the consultant did not have time to get a colleague to read it over), and the focus throughout any such document must be on the customer's needs and perceptions. Certainly once a proposal of yours has gone out, then you have to live with it. It is not going to sound very professional to telephone a correction later or send a revised 'page 7' to be slotted in by the prospect. With all that in mind, let us turn to see how the content should be arranged and dealt with in a proposal.

Proposal content

While the form and certainly the content of a proposal can vary, the main divisions are best described as:

- the introduction (often preceded by a contents page);
- the statement of need;
- the recommendations (or solution);

- areas of detail (such as costs, timing, logistics, technical specification);
- the closing statement (or summary);
- additional information (of prime or lesser importance – in the form of appendices).

Each may need a number of subheadings and their length may vary with context, but they form a convenient way of reviewing the key issues about the construction of a proposal and are thus commented on in turn below.

Contents page

A proposal of any complexity needs the equivalent of a book's title page. This states whom, or which organization, it is for, what it is about and whom it is from. This page can also give the contact details – address, etc – of the proposer (which if not here, must certainly be in the proposal somewhere) and some proposal writers like to feature the logo of the recipient organization on it, as well as his or her own.

A front sheet giving the contents and page numbers should follow this. It may make it look more interesting if there are sub-headings as well as main headings, especially if the main headings have to be bland, eg 'Introduction'. Action words – making, creating etc – should be preferred.

The headings that follow below are descriptive of the functions and role of the sections, not recommendations for headings you should necessarily use.

Introduction

Remember this is a sales document. The opening must command attention, establish interest and lead into the main text, making people want to read on. As the introduction has to undertake a number of important, yet routine, tasks, it may be best to start with a sentence (or more) that is interesting, rings bells with the customer and sets the tone for the document.

Thereafter, there are a number of other roles for the introduction. It may need, for instance, to:

- establish the background;
- refer to past meetings and discussions;
- recap decisions made to date;
- quote experience;
- acknowledge terms of reference;
- list the names of those involved in the discussions and/or preparation of the document.

As none of this is as interesting as what will follow, this section should concentrate on essentials and be kept short. The final words should act as a bridge to the next section.

Statement of need

This section needs to set out, with total clarity, the brief in terms of the needs of the customer. It describes the scope of the requirement and may well act to recap and confirm what it was agreed at a prior meeting that the proposal was intended to cover.

It is easy to ask why this should be necessary. Surely the customer knows what he or she wants? Indeed he or she has perhaps just spent a considerable amount of time telling you exactly that. But this statement is still important.

Its role is to make clear that you *do have complete understanding* of the situation. It emphasizes the identity of views between the two parties, and gives credibility to your later suggestions by making clear that they are based firmly on the real needs that exist. Without this it might be possible for the customer to assume that you are suggesting what is best (or perhaps most profitable) for you; or simply making a standard suggestion.

This section is also key if the proposal is to be seen by people who were not party to the original discussions; for them it may be the first clear statement of this picture.

Again, this part should link naturally into the next section.

Recommendations or solution

This may well be the longest section and needs to be logically arranged and divided (as do all the sections) to make it manageable. Here you state what you feel meets the requirements. This may be standard, in the sense that it is a list of, for example, recommended equipment and spares which are all items drawn from published information such as a catalogue. Or it may be bespoke, as with the approach a consultant might set out to instigate a process of change or implement training.

In either case this section needs to be set out in a way that is 'benefits-led', spelling out the advantages and making clear what the solution will mean to, or do for, the individual customer as well as specifying the technical features. If you are unfamiliar with the concept of benefits and features in terms of what makes a persuasive case, the boxed paragraph sets out a few details (though you could find more research is necessary here).

Describing benefits

Customers do not buy products and services for what they are, they buy them for what the products or services *do* for them or *mean* to them – for their *benefits*. They do not buy precision drills (what they are), but the ability to make precision holes (what drills will do); and they will only want that because of some deeper need, to repair the car or put up shelves. This is probably the single most important tenet of successful selling, yet the world over there are many sales people talking predominantly about *features* (those things that the product or a part of it *is*) when they should be talking benefits. And, as a result, there are potential buyers with their eyes glazing over saying to themselves 'So what?'

In a proposal talking benefits, and indeed leading with benefits, is key in making what you say attractive. It is not so complicated, yet perhaps because so many people take a rather introspective view of what their organization does, it takes conscious effort not to state things that way round.

The first task is to recognise which is which, feature or benefit, and it is useful to think through your product/service listing benefits first and seeing how they link with features. Consider a simple example: a car may have a six-speed gearbox (a feature); telling the customer this may seem just like another piece of technical information prompting that 'So what?' response. Worse, the inexperienced driver may worry that it is more complicated than they can manage. If the sales person has identified a need for economy, they can talk first about low fuel usage and money saved (benefits), quoting the feature of the six-speed gearbox as a reason for that being possible. One feature may, of course, link to more than one benefit. In the case of the car, reduced engine wear and smoother, quieter high speed cruising may also result from the six-speed gearbox. Try thinking this through with something a little more technical in mind (ABS brakes or torque, perhaps for the car) or applying it to your own product.

All product description can be handled in this way: thus a grill (designed for a restaurant) may be better described as being able to cook a dozen eggs at one time rather than saying it has a surface area some 300 square centimetres. Saying something about how it will cook not only allows a benefit to be described, it is also a much more descriptive way of putting it to any restaurateur – they can then see in their mind's eye how much easier that will be than the smaller model they have now and contemplate coping with the rush at breakfast more easily. It puts it in their terms.

Talking benefits in this way as you describe product, company, and the people and service that support them is a vital part of the task. It is important to get it right if a case is to be persuasive.

Remember too that all customers are different, and in some cases you may be selling to a group of people who *all* have influence on a decision, as with a board of directors. In either case people will have their own needs and agenda and benefits must be presented so that they relate to these individual situations and points of view. There is also research that shows that what works well is a 'Goldilocks' proposal – one with a number of key benefits that make a sound case, sufficient to persuade and without presenting such a long list that the detail begins to switch people off.

The whole area of persuasive techniques may need further study.

Remember, the sales job here is threefold: to explain, to do so persuasively and also to differentiate. Never forget, when putting together a proposal, that you may well be in competition and what you present will be compared with the offerings of others.

A focus on the customer's needs is usually the best way to ensure the readers' attention; nothing must be said that does not have a clear customer relevance. One further emphasis is particularly important here: individuality. It is very easy to store standard documents, and indeed it may be possible to edit one proposal into a new version that does genuinely suit a similar need elsewhere (but double, double check that you have changed the customer's name!). It must not seem standardized though. This is sufficiently important to re-emphasize: it must never seem standard in any sense. Customers may well know that you must get many similar requests, but will still appreciate clear signs that you have prepared something tailored just for them.

Only when this section has been covered thoroughly should you move on to costs. Only when the customer appreciates exactly what value and benefits are being provided can price be considered in context.

Costs

These must be stated clearly, not look disguised (though certain techniques for presenting the figures are useful, eg amortizing costs see Chapter 5).

All the necessary detail must be there, including any items that are:

- options;
- extras;
- associated expenses.

These must be shown and made clear. I know of one company that lost a contract when one of their executives met the Managing Director of the customer at a railway station and it was clear that all travel – which was agreed – was being billed for First Class – which had neither been discussed or specified.

This is no place for a treatise on pricing policy, but note that:

- price should be linked as closely as possible to benefits;
- this section must establish or reinforce that you offer value for money;
- invoicing details and trading terms often need including, and must always be clear; mistakes here tend to be expensive. (In the UK remember to make clear whether price is inclusive of VAT);
- overseas, attention must be given to currency considerations;
- comparisons may need to be made with the competition;
- range figures (necessary in some businesses) must be used carefully (you should never make the range gap too wide, or you lose credibility, and never pick an upper range figure that you might exceed; doing so is always much resented).

Look carefully at how you arrange this section. It is only realistic to assume that some readers will look at this before reading *anything else*. Certainly for them there need to be sufficient explanation, cost justification and – above all – clear benefits, linked in here. Just the bald figures can be very off-putting.

Areas of detail

There are additional topics that it may be necessary to deal with here (as mentioned above), such as timing, logistics, staffing, etc. Sometimes these are best combined with costs as one section. Not if there are too many, but for example, costs and timing go well together, with perhaps one other separate, numbered, section dealing with any final topics before moving on.

The principles here are similar to those for handling costs. Matters such as timing must be made completely clear and all possibilities of misunderstanding or omission avoided.

Summary or closing statement

The final section must act to round off the document and it has a number of specific jobs to do. Its first, and perhaps most important, task is to summarize. All the threads must be drawn together and key aspects emphasized. This fulfils a number of purposes:

- It is a useful conclusion for all readers and should ensure the proposal ends on a note that they can easily agree is an effective summary. Because this is often the most difficult part of the document to write, it is also a part that can impress disproportionately. Readers know good summarizing is not easy and they respect the writer who achieves it.

- It is useful too in influencing others, around the decision maker, who may study the summary but not go through the whole proposal in detail.

- It ensures the final word, and the final impression left with the reader, is about benefits and value for money.

In addition, it can be useful to:

- recap key points (as well as key benefits);
- stress that the proposals are, in effect, the mutual conclusions of both parties (if this is so);
- link to action, action dates and points and people of contact (though this could equally be dealt with in the covering letter);
- invoke a sense of urgency (you will normally hope for things to be tied down promptly, but ultimately must respect the prospect's timing).

Remember that this summary may have to work in concert with the so-called 'executive summary', which is placed at the start of the document to do much the same job.

How to use appendices

The key thing here is appendices. It is important that proposals, like any document, flow. The argument they present must proceed logically and there must be no distractions from the developing picture. Periodically, there is sometimes a need to go into deep detail. Especially if this is technical, tedious or if it involves numerous figures – however necessary the content may be – it is better not to let such detail slow and interrupt the flow of the argument. Such information can usefully be referred to at the appropriate point, but with a note that the 'chapter and verse' is in an appendix. Be specific, saying for example: 'This detail will be found in Appendix 2: Costs and timing, which appears on page 21.' This arrangement can be used for a variety of elements: terms of reference, contract details, worked examples, graphs and figures, tables and so on.

Each of the major sections should be appropriately and, if possible, interestingly titled and you may sensibly start each main section on a new page, certainly with a proposal of any length.

Language and layout are important throughout, and comment about both appears in their respective chapters.

Checklist

Before writing a proposal, or to assist critique of one, ask yourself:

- Has the appropriate format (letter or formal) been chosen?
- Will it meet the needs of all involved (eg decision makers, recommenders, influencers)?
- Does the introduction include:
  - something to generate early interest?
  - appropriate reference back?
  - a clear description of purpose?
  - a clear, and individual, customer orientation?
- Does the statement of need include:
  - a clear picture of the prospect's situation and needs?
  - specific links between the prospect's needs and recommendations or suggestions to come?
  - reference to the prospect's decision criteria?
- Do the recommendations or solution include:
  - clear and specific recommendations (and sufficient options if appropriate)?
  - the relationship of recommendations to needs?
  - a statement of how recommendations meet the buying criteria?
  - reference to benefits (and in the right proportion to features)?
  - evidence or proof to establish credibility?
- Do price statements:
  - link to benefits (tangible or not)?
  - include *everything* that will affect cost?
  - *not* appear other than straightforward?
  - justify cost where necessary?

- present them as advantageously as possible (eg amortizing if appropriate)?
- Does the closing statement:
  - offer an impressive summary?
  - tie up all loose ends?
  - link specifically to action?
- What about any final elements? Are all appendices, attachments (eg brochures, fact sheets, exhibits) checked and complete?
- Is the covering letter really *adding* something to the total message?

Covering letters

Picking up the last question above, the quality of covering letters is worth emphasizing. Such a letter is important. It should do more than just say 'The proposal is enclosed', yet this is often all it does.

The covering letter is an opportunity. A good letter can:

- exemplify and emphasize elements of the proposal (and even repeat key points);
- say something about the organization and the people;
- link to the circumstances (for example, stating that another meeting is needed, showing how it can be useful and even acting to help set it up);
- enhance the appearance of the total package;
- act, not least, as a courtesy.

An example will help make this clear, and also emphasizes and exemplifies the nature of persuasive writing compared with a standardized and administratively oriented approach.

The following letter (on pages 114–15) came after I had telephoned a major hotel, enquiring about the possibility of booking space for a training course. It is a simple example, but came with a brochure and other details: a package very much akin to a proposal and with more details of potential costs than are in the letter.

The proposal element of this was a bound pack setting out the full 'facilities' (what an unattractive word), with 36 suggested menus, forms to complete specifying detailed requirements, and more.

Let us concentrate on the letter. It is not untypical of this field. It sounds well intentioned, polite and it gives a little information.

Otherwise it is wholly awful. Ignoring the finer points (and the punctuation), the following points come immediately to mind (commenting down the page):

- I do not want to hear about their delight (of course, they want my business); starting with something about me, my needs and circumstances would be better.

- I am not running a 'meeting and luncheon' – I explained it was a training session – this is their terminology not mine (and immediately shows the letter is standard).

SAMPLE LETTER

Dear Mr Forsyth,

Following my telephone call with you yesterday, I was delighted to hear of your interest in our hotel for a proposed meeting and luncheon some time in the future.

I have pleasure in enclosing for your perusal our banqueting brochure together with the room plan and, as you can see, some of our rooms could prove ideal for your requirements.

At this stage, I would be more than happy to offer you our delegate rate of... [*so much*]... to include the following:

- morning coffee with biscuits
- 3-course luncheon with coffee
- afternoon tea with biscuits
- overhead projector and flipchart
- pads and pencils
- room hire
- service and tax

and I trust this meets with your approval.

Should you at any time wish to visit our facilities and discuss your requirements further, please do not hesitate to contact me but, in the meantime, if you have any queries on the above, I would be pleased to answer them.

Yours sincerely

- The training session is not 'some time in the future', I quoted a date.

- Next they express more pleasure. I am more interested in what receiving the brochure will do for me, rather than in what sending it does for them (and yes, people really do use the word perusal in writing, though it seems very old fashioned and would not, I think, be used in speech).

- Also, although the room plan is useful, I do not see this as a banquet and the phrase 'banqueting brochure' does not seem right – it is their jargon not mine.

- The section about costs begins 'At this stage…' which seems to imply 'later we might negotiate something different' (even if they would, I am sure they did not mean to suggest this); and are costs best described with the hope that they 'meet with my approval'?

- Offering to arrange a viewing is surely what most prospects would want and should be set out as a firm offer, made easy, and positioned as the natural way forward.

- Talking about 'queries' implies fault (it would be better to offer additional information).

- The conclusion is weak and leaves the action with the recipient.

One could go on. The overall impression is introspective, standard, formulistic and it added little or nothing to the simple proposal sent; in fact it lessened it.

It is worth a short digression to stress the point about being introspective, or rather *not* being introspective (see page 117).

SAMPLE LETTER: AN ALTERNATIVE APPROACH

Dear Mr Forsyth,

Training seminar: venue arrangements to make your meeting work well

Your training seminar would, I am sure, go well here. Let me explain why. From how you described the event, you need a business-like environment, no distractions, all the necessary equipment and everything the venue does to run like clockwork.

Our XXX room is among a number regularly and successfully used for this kind of meeting. It is currently available on the dates you mentioned: 3–4 July. As an example, one package that suits many organizers is:

- morning tea/coffee and biscuits
- 3-course lunch with tea/coffee
- afternoon tea/coffee and biscuits
- pads, pencils and name cards for each participant
- room hire (including the use of an OHP and flipchart)

at a cost of xxx per head including service and tax.

Alternatively, you may wish to discuss other options; our main concern is to meet your specific needs and get every detail just right.

You will almost certainly want to see any room suggested; perhaps I may telephone you to set up a convenient time for you to come in and have a look. Meantime, our meetings brochure is enclosed (you will see our XXX room on page 3). This, and the room plan enclosed with our full proposals, will enable you to begin to plan how your meeting would work here.

Thank you for thinking of us; I look forward to speaking to you again soon.

Yours sincerely

Avoiding introspection

An example quickly shows how inappropriate an introspective approach is, where every thought is presented from the perspective of the writer. The following uses my own firm as an example:

The firm

- Touchstone Training & Consultancy was formed in 1990 to specialize in offering training in marketing and communications skills.
- We pride ourselves on offering a very practical approach.
- Our services range from courses on business writing (including report writing) to helping develop presentational skills for individuals.
- We are pleased to discuss your requirements with no obligation and use an initial meeting to ensure that a tailored solution is prepared for you.

Although there is a degree of information here, for instance knowing a firm has been operating for quite a number of years indicates that probably it has been doing something right, the net effect of such an approach is bland and seems to lack connection with potential clients; it also allows questions that highlight its inadequacy such as what's a 'practical approach'? I will resist transforming this into a sales pitch; suffice to say that information focused on and phrased from the readers' point of view is likely to work much better, for example here starting by writing about what better communication can achieve and only then how we might help achieve that. This concept, and the positive side of it, is investigated further in the context of covering letters (persuasive letters to accompany proposals).

So, having been just somewhat critical I suppose I must attempt to balance the picture. The letter can doubtless be improved further, but I would certainly have regarded something like the letter on page 116 as much more appropriate. The greatest difference is the improved focus on the customer.

This starts with a statement with which surely all meeting organizers would identify (it is designed to get them saying 'That's exactly what I want' and feeling that the writer understands their point of view). It is much more conversational and has an altogether better 'feel'. Interestingly, small changes make a difference: for example, leave the word 'just' out of the sentence after the list and it does not sound as appropriate. The letter is important, and more so for more complex situations and more elaborate proposals than the above. It will, if it is interesting, likely be the first thing that is read. It sets the scene for the rest of the message.

This aspect should never be handled just as a routine, administrative, matter. It does, or should do, a part of the persuasive job that writing any sort of proposal entails. Miss out on making the covering letter informative and impressive and you risk diluting the whole case – perhaps significantly.

Assuming proposals arrive safely and are read, there is another possibility that needs some thought.

The presentation of proposals

Some proposals are posted just like a letter; once in front of the prospect they must do their work alone, though they may be followed up in numerous ways, by letter, telephone, etc (persistence here can pay dividends).

Note: Think carefully about emailing proposals; something I observe increasingly being done automatically and thus with little or no thought about how it appears. There are several potential hazards here. For example, a client may print out a proposal in black and miss completely what you have carefully emphasized in colour, fail to circulate to colleagues in the right way or read it on screen, a process that, as has been said, risks diluting understanding. Of course they should arrive efficiently and in good time. But an email can be deleted in a split second and may not look as smartly presented as a mailed printed copy. Also it may not be forwarded to everyone involved in a decision. Ask about this by all means and email if that method of delivery is selected, but be sure you know how many copies are needed and consider sending (by mail, courier or whatever timing dictates) smartly printed copies as well.

Often complex proposals, especially those involving more than one person in the decision, will be the subject of formal presentations. These can happen in two main ways: either the proposal is sent and a presentation is made later to those who have (or should have!) read the document; or the presentation is made first, with the detailed proposal being left as a permanent reminder of the presentation's content.

If such an arrangement is made in advance, then the proposal needs to reflect what it is. For example, you may need more detail in a proposal that has to stand on its own than in one that follows a presentation. It might sometimes be possible (with the prospect's agreement) to delay completing the proposal until after a presentation, allowing the inclusion of any final elements stemming from any feedback arising during the presentation.

There should be a close parallel between the two entities so that it is clear how anything said at a presentation relates to the proposal. Rarely will any of the proposal be read out verbatim. Indeed, other than for very short extracts, it probably should not be. People listening with a document in front of them are almost always distracted by the text they see (and people can read much faster to themselves than you can out loud so they get ahead, miss any emphasis you may give and find what is happening annoying). However, additional explanation, examples and exemplification of what has been written are important.

It may cause confusion if, say, a proposal with eight main headings is discussed at a meeting with nine or ten items being run through (certainly without explanation). It is helpful to the proposer if the job of preparing the proposal and the presentation overlap and are kept close.

A final idea here may be useful: more than one company I know print out – for themselves – a 'presentation copy' of the proposal in a larger format or type size. This enables it to be easily read by someone making a presentation and thus usually standing up. It gives additional space to annotate the document with any notes that will help guide the presentation along precisely.

Earn attention

The secret of a good proposal is in attention to detail and care in preparation (leaving the obvious necessity of meeting customer needs in terms of the message on one side). As a final comment I cannot resist referring to the Video Arts training film *The Proposal* (which I can certainly highly recommend).

The film shows a salesman struggling to complete a proposal. He daydreams of the rapturous reception with which the buyer will greet the arrival of his deathless prose and the certainty of an order to follow. But the voice-over interrupts – 'but it's not like that is it?' – and his vision changes to a less rosy image. This time when the proposal is delivered, we see the buyer (John Cleese) sitting at his desk, a picture of hungover misery. He is slowly dropping Alka-Seltzer tablets into a glass and wincing at the fizzing noise they make.

There can be few better images to have in mind when you sit down to write a proposal. If you aim to make your next one combat that sort of barrier, you will have to think carefully about it and invest it with some power.

Exercise

Again it may be useful to check your own work here; clearly it is important not only that a proposal reads well but that it is truly likely to persuade. As an additional thought, check the weight of the argument: recent research shows that not only are too few points designed to give weight and credibility being used, which is likely to weaken a case, but also that too many points can be seen as boring, inappropriate or suggest desperation, especially if endless minor 'advantages' are listed en masse. Though there may be exceptions, in terms of key points, the best number seems to be between five and seven.

Summary points

- Always remember that reports and proposals are distinct from each other.
- Make sure a proposal reflects the identified need of the prospect/customer.
- Do not be introspective; the job is to persuade and this necessitates a customer focus.
- A proposal very likely must set you apart from any competition as well as say that what you offer is good.
- Always link the proposal tightly to subsequent action.
- Do not just write a proposal well; package and present it well too.

07

The contribution of layout and presentation

The way a report or proposal looks is important. It influences a number of things, ranging from whether it is read, and how carefully it is read, to the frame of mind in which it is read. It should be said at once that prevailing presentational standards have increased dramatically in this respect in recent years. Modern equipment, computers, laser printers and so on mean that very professional results are possible for even the smallest company. If you want something printed in colour, if you want a table turned into a graph of some sort, then both these things and more can be achieved at the touch of a button. Even if there is a learning curve involved, most people are gradually getting more and more able to use the sorts of abilities modern equipment makes possible – even if the technology moves ahead as you watch, and makes it a continuing task.

Whatever the level of complexity you need, however, you should be aware that those who are going to be on the receiving end of your writing doubtless receive other documents on a regular basis. If the standard of those is high, and it is likely to be, then yours must look as good, or better.

Again there is no one magic formula for success, rather a number of different things to keep in mind and a number of devices from which to select. All are concerned primarily with enhancing clarity or producing appropriate emphasis. This chapter therefore reviews a range of overall presentational factors. There is no suggestion here, incidentally, that every report or proposal should incorporate all of these. Indeed, such devices should not be over-used or the net effect can become messy, and useful emphasis can then turn into something that appears strident and inappropriate.

Before we get into the areas this element of a document implies, consider this: most people do not read a business report or pro-posal carefully line by line. They read the first part – a few lines or a bit more – and then start to scan. The way the document is pre-sented, and the graphic variety and emphasis, make it more likely that they will slow and take in important points of what you are trying to put across.

In case you doubt just how important it is to prompt attention, consider one piece of research. Professor Colin Mason of the University of Southampton headed some research into how thor-oughly potential investors read the marketing plans of businesses in which they considered taking a stake. These are important docu-ments and typically (in the ones used in the study) were 60 pages in length. Yet the average time spent studying them was a mere eight minutes; hardly long enough for a careful read, much less a lengthy study. Other studies, I am thinking of one about how employers study CVs, support this view.

Your documents really must earn a reading and they must do so quickly. The early part of the text is important, so too is how they look and how easy it is to pick up clues and focus on particular areas that seem of interest within the text. That being so, let's see how specifically presentation contributes.

There are four main areas requiring attention here: the graphics and layout of the page; the use of exhibits (like graphs or charts); options that suit certain circumstances (like appendices); and the overall packaging (binding, etc) of the document.

How the pages look

The first thing to be mentioned here is, in fact, nothing.

The white space of the page is as important as what is on it. If text is densely packed, it seems to have no space to breathe, one thing runs into the next and any intended emphasis is diluted or lost. In addition, it simply looks off-putting and will seem, and be, harder to read.

So the first rule of layout is to space things out. In a long report especially, all the spaces between headings and sections, and even between paragraphs, need to be sufficient to give the right look. Margins should not be set too tight. Remember that many recipients of these documents tend to annotate them. What looks neat and tidy on arrival, may look a real mess when someone has been through it to prepare for a meeting, say. Assume this will be done and leave enough space for it to be done conveniently.

Now we look, in turn, at a number of different aspects of what is on the pages and how it is arranged.

Page layout

The specimen page (shown on pages 125–27) illustrates just a few of the ways of laying out a document. These days many such formats can be called up as integral parts of a word processing system; the permutations are numerous. It is also easy to modify such standard offerings, or indeed to create new formats, so you should be sure you select something that is just right for your purpose.

Specimen page

1. INTRODUCTION

This page is presented to give some examples of the many possibilities available. As it needs some text, it highlights some of the key elements that layout can incorporate. These are referred to in more detail in the text.

2. KEY ELEMENTS

Headings need to stand out. It makes it easier to scan a page and pick out specific items or topics. In addition, bullet points are useful to highlight subheadings, used here to flag other ways of creating graphic emphasis:

- **bold type**: text in **bold type stands out** even in the middle of a line; this is not only for headings.
- CAPITAL LETTERS are also useful.

Alternatively, lists can be made easier to read simply by putting each item on a new line, perhaps started by a dash or short rule:

- this differentiates points from the main text;
- it also groups items that naturally sit together.

Such a list could open with: 'There are three key factors here...' And you can number them:

1 First, there is...

2 Second, there is...

3 And so on.

Dividing a section

Sometimes if the main numbered headings are too long they need to be subdivided. This is easily done with subheadings such as the one preceding this paragraph. Other factors can act in a similar way.

> **For example, a key sentence may be indented like this, this stands out at once; bold type reinforces the effect.**

Shown here sandwiched between lines of routine text, the effect is very clear.*

3. FINALLY

Just to complete, and fill, this page it should be noted that the example given relates to overall layout, and it is *not* usually appropriate to have so many different devices as there are on this page in such a short space. The effect, if these elements are overdone, can become messy.

This could also be in, say, italics. (Footnotes can be useful.)

Typeface

The options here are again many. It may be useful to chop and change in various ways, but using too many typefaces in any one document quickly makes it untidy.

Most organizations adopt a standard layout (or layouts) and this is something that is designed, not least, to blend in well with the style of their letterheads and reflect corporate image and style. A consistent look is sensible if a number of items are all going to end up in the same place, say in a customer's file.

Type size

This can be varied to a greater extent than typefaces. Larger and smaller sizes may be usefully picked to do particular jobs, for example:

larger for title pages or headings;

smaller for footnotes or asides of lesser importance.

Graphic emphasis

There are a number of ways to make a part of the text stand out, or, for that matter push other parts into the background (some of these link to the page layout examples):

- CAPITAL LETTERS;
- **bold type** (which can be used to highlight a word or sentence in the text, as well as for headings: see specimen page);
- *italics*;
- underlining;
- indenting. Indenting is often used with bullet points, and as well as the 'standard bullet' there are several designs: one to match every style of document.

None of these devices are mutually exclusive, something can be in **BOLD CAPITALS**, in <u>UNDERLINED CAPITALS</u> (or both) or whatever other permutation suits and does the job.

> Another device is the boxed paragraph. This is useful for asides, something that is not so dependent on the sequence involved, summaries – or whatever needs a higher degree of separation. The boxed paragraphs in this series are typical examples.

Numbering

It is important for readers to be able to find their way easily around a document. Not just through it, but back and forth if they want to locate a particular item.

Pages should always be numbered, probably headings too. Subheadings can be numbered also, of course, though the use of bullet points may reduce the need for some of this. Formal numbering can also be used thus:

1 For main headings, 1.1, 1.2, 1.3 etc for subheadings, or even for paragraphs. (This is not suitable for everything as it appears formal and has a touch of the old style civil service about it.)

There are a number of ways of numbering as well as 1., 2., 3. These include i), ii), iii); a), b), c); A, B, C; thus it is possible to have a hierarchy of numbered points without instigating any confusion. Always check carefully and be consistent in the way you do this. Also double-check that when you say something such as *There are three key points here*, you do stop at three. This is easily missed as your thoughts run on (if you spot an example in this book, let me know!).

The rule here is that complexity dictates practice. If something is long and complicated then the numbering will have to be extra clear. This is also important if you know a lot of discussion will be held while referring to the document.

New pages

You may elect to have each main heading starting on a new page (or not, it can look odd and wasteful if this results in too many white spaces).

Example

A firm of architects habitually produced proposals with many – and impressive – illustrations, something by no means unique to this sector of business.

In order to make them even more impressive the architects doubled the size of their whole proposal document (up from A4). They then checked the response to this with some simple research and found that prospects and clients did not appreciate their carefully prepared documents. Why not? For the simple reason that they no longer fitted in a conventional filing system. This meant they caused problems and, for all their visual excellence, were too often seen as inconvenient or even a nuisance.

The moral: creativity always needs to come second to clarity and convenience – for the customer. In this case the proposers reverted to the original format.

The exhibits

Because not everything can be expressed best in words, a number of devices are available to create greater clarity. Some of these, like bar charts, are concerned with projecting numbers and financial information, which was dealt with in Chapter 5. The following range across the kind of things that can be used.

Project timetables

A device to help people visualize the timescale of projects with multiple and overlapping stages.

A	Phase 1	2	3	4
B	1	2	3	
C	1	2	3	4	5

—————————— Time ——————————→

Flowchart

This is more complex, or rather it is for expressing a more complex picture. Best to express interrelationships.

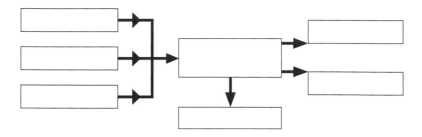

Organizational charts

These may represent the whole organization, or simply a project team. It usually describes a hierarchy, but this need not be people.

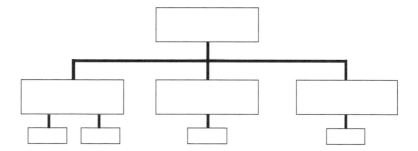

Pictures

Pictures are not appropriate everywhere, but if there is a role for them then they can work well. They are best with captions, and should be positioned accurately to fit in appropriately with the sense of the text.

All of these devices benefit by being kept as simple as possible. Two exhibits of some sort often work better than one over-elaborate one. Using more than one colour can add clarity (even if other pages of a report are black and white) and is increasingly being used as printer costs come down and quality goes up. Remember, however, that simply adding a second colour will not in any way compensate for a lack of substance in the written message.

Sometimes there is a compromise here between 'perfection' and the additional time taken to produce exhibits of this sort. If clarity is at risk without them, do take the time; it might make all the difference to the result.

Other options for inclusion

Appendices were mentioned in the chapter on proposals. I will not repeat what was said there, except to say that the key role of such items is to keep long detailed items separate from the main flow of the content. The more technical and the more detailed such items are, the more important it is to separate them from the main text.

Whatever they are and however many of them there may be, they must be as well presented as the rest of the document. Indeed if they are adding fine detail, then they may need particular attention. Not only typed and printed material may be appended in this way. Additional material, everything from photocopies of press clippings to technical literature and brochures, can entirely legitimately be included. The only criterion is that the recipient will see it as necessary and suitable in whatever form it is added.

Certain documents need an index. This is not so common as the need to include a title page and/or contents page (both mentioned with reference to proposals). The key point to be sure of is that readers will never be flicking to and fro through the pages, wondering why there is not more guidance as to how to find particular items.

Overall packaging

Reports and proposals cannot be sent as an unattached bundle of loose papers. How they are secured affects their presentation, therefore the method chosen is dictated by the need to impress the reader. Convenience is also a factor, and many people favour binding systems that allow the report to be opened and lie flat unaided. This makes sense and is especially appreciated if someone is trying to write on the document to add their own comments.

There are several options:

- A simple report sent to colleagues may only need a staple in the top left-hand corner.

- The report can be clipped into a standard report cover or ring binder (one option here is to have a transparent plastic cover that allows the top sheet to be on letterhead or for a smart title page to show through). There are many different types of fastening systems.

- The report can be bound using something like a plastic or wire spine with a cover that can be personalized to identify the organization, department or sender.

There are many options here, so it is partly a matter of taste. However, do not go on using an aged and unsuitable binding machine just because it is there. Select something suitable – maybe you need several different methods depending on the recipient – and finish the whole job off well. One or two small final points: if the report is going in the mail, select a smart envelope if you want it to impress. Certainly select something that will get it to its destination in good condition. Do not forget to weigh a heavy document. If you guess the amount and end up with your best customer paying the excess charge, it will not put them in the best mood to read whatever you have sent. Think also about the urgency of it – should it go in the post or by courier or some sort of express dispatch service?

If your next important document arrives on time and looking good that is one hurdle over. Beyond that it must earn a reading; and then reward it.

Exercise

As a final check, one which may initially take no more than a glance if you have been turning to one of your own reports or proposals as you have been reading, consider how your document(s) look. That is, you should consider how they will appear to a reader. The first check should be for clarity. Does it look easy to read and understand? The second is for appropriate professionalism. Does it reflect the image you want to project? Be sure that embellishments do not overpower content or understanding and that the content and readability is as good as the look. It may well need to look as if trouble has been taken over it but it will wisely not look too over the top; if the impression is given that more time and trouble has been given to the look than the content that will not score you points. Too much embellishment can put people off. (Writing this reminds me of someone I heard saying that you should 'never do business with a company that has a fountain in their reception area'; meaning that any image they project should be closely linked to practicalities and that any inappropriate overspending is coming from customers. There is a moral here for written communication too, I think.)

Summary points

- Make sure the page layout is appropriate to the purpose and the reader.

- Make sure the detail of the layout provides clear signposting to content.

- Use graphic devices to ensure precise emphasis is where you want it.

- Create suitable illustrations (graphs, charts, etc) to assist explanation.

- Keep detailed matters separate (eg in an appendix) to maintain the flow.

- Package the whole thing for convenience and to give the right impression.

AFTERWORD

What is written without effort is in general read without pleasure.
SAMUEL JOHNSON

Business writing and the most complex form of it, writing reports and proposals, is not something most people who work in organizations can avoid. It goes with the territory, as they say. Given that it must be done, there are only really two options. The first is to do it well, in which case you will make what you write have the greatest likelihood of achieving what you want.

The second is to muddle through, regarding it as a chore, getting by, and perhaps missing the opportunities the process presents. In some ways the second option seems almost attractive. Some people persuade themselves that the effort of doing otherwise is not worthwhile or is too time-consuming. Some remain convinced they cannot change what they regard as a 'fixed' style. But for most a little thought quickly shows that the second is not really an option at all.

There is regularly too much hanging on the job that reports and proposals must do to treat them other than seriously. If results are not to suffer and if your profile, and prospects, as the writer are to be as you wish, writing good reports and proposals is something that demands attention.

It does not just happen, of course, and is easy to understate or underestimate. (I have seen it said that writing is easy, all you need to do is think of all the words you know and put some of them down in the right order.) It certainly requires some effort, especially if you feel set in your ways. But all the factors that make for success are essentially common sense. Preparation is key. A sound, logical structure creates a core that carries the content and begins to make a message clear and attractive. Language matters too.

If you have clear objectives and say what you mean, succinctly, and build in appropriate description and style, people are more likely to want to read.

Bearing these principles in mind, any necessary new habits can quickly build up to replace old ones. You will find that with some consideration and practice you will write more easily, more certainly, and in a way that is well matched to your purpose and to your intended readers. This, in turn, will make it more likely that you will achieve your objectives. Even the best writing will not rescue a poor case, but it will strengthen whatever case you put over, making it more likely to be studied, considered and acted on in the way you intend.

With practice you will also find that such writing takes less time. Good preparation particularly can remove the need for elaborate rewriting and editing on material that should have been closer to its aim in the first place, if only it had been given more thought. If writing can be achieved promptly, it becomes less of a chore and this may itself act to allow you to think about it in the right way.

After all, there is a certain pleasure in finding what you consider just the right phrase to make a point; more in finding it has worked and been well received. Professional writers, no doubt, suffer as much as anyone in trying to get down what they want in a way they are happy with. But they also report it to be a satisfying process, even if this is with hindsight: one writer, Michael Kanin, is quoted as saying, 'I don't like to write, but I love to have written.'

So the next document you have to write presents a particular opportunity. Having read this book, you will know something of the factors that help create good business writing. Whatever your current style and standard, there may be new things you can try, old things you can aim to change and improve.

Two things in conclusion: first, some reminders (see box), then...

Some writing rules

Various versions of the following rules may be seen posted on office walls. All twist the language to make a point in an amusing way and thus help make the rule memorable.

- Don't abbrev things inappropriately.
- Check to see if you any words out.
- Be careful to use adjectives and adverbs correct.
- About sentences fragments.
- Don't use no double negatives.
- Just between you and I, case is important.
- Join clauses good, like a conjunction should.
- Don't use commas, that aren't necessary.
- Its important to use apostrophe's right.
- It's better not to unnecessarily split infinitives.
- Only Proper Nouns should be capitalized. also a sentence should begin with a capital and end with a full stop
- Use hyphens in compound-words, not just in any two-word phrase.
- In letters reports and things like that we use commas to keep a string of items apart.
- Watch out for irregular verbs that have creeped into your language.
- Verbs has to agree with their subjects.
- A writer mustn't change your point of view.
- A preposition isn't a good thing to end a sentence with.
- Avoid clichés like the plague.

I will give the last word to an especially prolific author, Isaac Asimov (who wrote nearly 500 books, mainly science and science fiction). Asked what he would do if told he only had six months to live, he answered simply: 'Type faster.' Clearly he was someone who enjoyed writing. But his reply is also a good example of the power of language. Think how much his response says about the man and his attitude to life, his work and his readers; and in just two words. The language you use can act powerfully for you and, provided it is well considered, can help you achieve much.

Postscript

Often proposals and presentations must act in tandem to make a successful case. A good proposal, and the thinking that produces it, can assist in preparing a good presentation, but equally the effectiveness of a good proposal can be diluted or ruined by a lacklustre presentation. Given this link, it seems appropriate to mention another book I have written for Kogan Page titled *The PowerPoint Detox*. It addresses the problem of what has become known as 'death by PowerPoint', the fact that too many presentations have become a dreary parade of lengthy text slides, too often read verbatim by the presenter, who at worst looks over their shoulder and away from the audience to do so. It suggests approaches to avoid this habit, which at best can dilute the power of a presentation, at worst kill it stone dead, and offers ways to enliven presentations.

Often reports and presentations go together. The book makes mention of reports and proposals, citing the occasion when poor slides, especially those with too much dense text, are poor because they are in fact simply pages, or sections of pages, lifted straight from a document. Not doing that is one message of the book; slides deserve to be tailor made so that they do a good job as a slide.

It is worth making the same point here, in reverse. In writing reports and proposals write what will create good pages for a report or proposal. Do not be tempted to tinker with what you know will be ideal for the page in an attempt to short cut the production of a parallel slide. You may know both are necessary. But slides and report pages are different things; they do different jobs and each must suit their particular task. Trying to combine the tasks just ensures you end up with a poor slide and an inadequate report. Keep them separate and make them both good.

Lightning Source UK Ltd.
Milton Keynes UK
UKHW051512070719
345645UK00006B/34/P